Essential Freud

CHRISTOPHER BADCOCK

ESSENTIAL FREUD

Basil Blackwell

First published 1988

Reprinted 1989

Basil Blackwell Ltd
108 Cowley Road, Oxford OX4 1JF, UK

Basil Blackwell Inc.
432 Park Avenue South, Suite 1503
New York, NY 10016, USA

British Library Cataloguing in Publication Data

Badcock, Christopher
  Essential Freud: a modern introduction
  to classical psychoanalysis.
  1. Freud, Sigmund   2. Psychoanalysis
  1. Title
  150.19′ 52   BF173.F85
  ISBN 0–631–15793–X
  ISBN 0–631–16413–8 Pbk

Library of Congress Cataloging in Publication Data

Badcock, C. R.
  Essential Freud: a modern introduction to classical
  psychoanalysis / Christopher Badcock.
  p.   cm.
  Bibliography: p.
  Includes index.
  ISBN 0–631–15793–X
  ISBN 0–631–16413–8 Pbk
  1. Psychoanalysis.   2. Freud, Sigmund. 1856–1939.   I.
Title.
  BF173.B147   1988
  150.19′ 52–dc19

Typeset in 11 on 13pt Bembo
by Columns of Reading
Printed in Great Britain by
Billing and Sons Ltd, Worcester

To my students

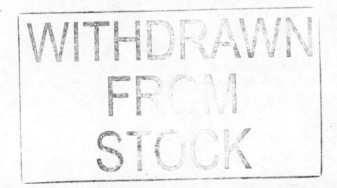

Contents

Preface

In my view there is but one way to bring a great scientist to the attention of the larger public: it is to discuss and explain, in language which will be generally understood, the problems and the solutions which have characterized his lifework. This can only be done by someone who has a fundamental grasp of the material . . . the external life and personal relations can only be, in the main, of secondary importance. Of course, in such a book, the personal side must be taken account of; but it should not be made the chief thing . . . Otherwise, the result is a banal hero-worship, based on emotion and not on insight. I have learned by my own experience how hateful and ridiculous it is, when a serious man, absorbed in important endeavours, is ignorantly lionized.[*]

Albert Einstein

I came across these words of Einstein's, addressed to someone who had asked him to contribute a foreword to a biography, as I was writing the last few pages of this book. Nothing could sum up better the approach to Freud which I have followed here. Like Einstein, I believe that it is the scientific content of psychoanalysis which matters, not minor biographical details, especially since the present work is not intended to be any kind of biography of Freud, but an introduction to his work.

[*]Quoted in B. Hoffman, *Albert Einstein: Creator and Rebel* (London, 1972), p. 10.

Readers will find that it is quite unlike any other such introduction, and may even give the impression of consciously setting out to do the exact opposite of what is customary. So, whereas most other introductions to psychoanalysis are heavily biographical and closely tied to Freud's original texts, this one contains a bare minimum of biography and avoids quotation, preferring an approach based on concepts and essentials. Again, whereas most other books reflect the biographical circumstance that psychoanalysis was discovered in the course of Freud's long career as a psychotherapist, this one avoids individual psychopathology and well-known case histories wherever possible and instead focuses on everyday, 'normal' examples, many of them drawn from my own experience and from my family. Unlike every other writer on the subject known to me except Freud himself, I have used examples of my own dreams rather than relying on second-hand material quoted from elsewhere. Finally, whereas most other approaches to Freud and psychoanalysis take the literary/artistic approach, mine ignores it for a resolutely scientific one, based in part on a comparison with Einstein and relativity.

The justification for such a parallel will appear in due course, but for the present let me point out that this book had two quite distinct sources of inspiration. One was a number of years' experience trying to teach the fundamentals of Freudian psychoanalysis to students at the London School of Economics; the other was a reading of a number of lay introductions to Einstein and relativity. In the course of reading these I found myself asking why someone could not write an introduction to Freud in the same way – especially since the conceptual problems seemed very comparable and the importance of psychoanalysis was only equalled in my view by the work of Einstein in twentieth-century science.

As a non-member of the official psychoanalytic establishment, I have tried to present Freud's work in a wider context than has become customary. Freud, who, by his own admission, was 'not a therapeutic enthusiast' and became a therapist against his will,★ took a rather less narrow view of his own creation than has been characteristic of most of the organized psychoanalytic movement, which has projected an image which is predominantly therapeutic and related to the personal concerns of the individual client. Here I have emphasized the converse: the general relevance of psychoanalysis to everyday life and to normality, as well as to groups and society at large. Wherever possible I have avoided jargon, but provided a glossary of unavoidable technical terms with simple definitions.

Although it is primarily intended for a lay readership and assumes absolutely no prior knowledge of the subject, I hope that this book, in view of its unusual approach and novel emphasis, may interest those with a professional interest in, or advanced knowledge of, Freud and psycho-analysis. I have been at some pains to attack what I regard as the completely false perspective with which Freud's work – particularly on child-development – is seen, especially by those in the behavioural and human sciences who should know better. Writing in 1915, Freud could say: 'Because no one is inclined to dispute constitutional factors, it devolves upon psychoanalysis to represent forcefully the interests of early infantile acquisitions.'† Yet today, when constitutional factors are routinely denied in favour of environmental, acquired ones, such an emphasis in his original writings is likely to be misunderstood.

In emphasizing the dynamic aspect as opposed to the environmental, I have attempted to redress the balance somewhat and to contradict the wide tendency to regard Freud as just another environmental determinist. In the chapters devoted to the Oedipus complex and the libido

★*New Introductory Lectures on Psychoanalysis, The Standard Edition of the Complete Psychological Works of Sigmund Freud* (London, 1953–1974), vol. XXII, p. 151; *The Complete Letters of Sigmund Freud to Wilhelm Fliess*, ed. J. Masson (Cambridge, Mass., 1985), p. 180.
†S. Freud, *A Phylogenetic Fantasy* (Cambridge, Mass., 1987), p.10.

theory I have gone some way beyond Freud's original mode of presentation and put his findings in the altogether more modern context of the theory of parental investment, which has been so widely influential in bringing a dynamic view of parent–offspring relations to biology. Finally, in my concluding remarks I have tried to look ahead to what may well be the eventual place of Freud's work in the science of the future. As I shall try to show, this vision of the future is not entirely speculative, but is already beginning to unfold.

The book is dedicated to my students, who taught me a great deal about how to present – and how not to present, which is perhaps more important – this kind of material. For a number of years they rehearsed me in the role of teacher of psychoanalysis, and anything which succeeds in this book is likely to be indebted to their influence on my presentation and choice of material.

I owe everything I know about psychoanalysis which I did not teach myself to my analyst and teacher, Anna Freud, and have a debt of gratitude to my wife for her helpful comments on the manuscript and to my sons for the many anecdotes about them within its pages. I must also acknowledge a special indebtedness to the works of Serge Moscovici for many important insights contained in the chapters dealing with Freud's mass psychology.

I must thank my publisher, John Davey, for his inestimable help, advice and encouragement throughout, and Sam Dorrance of Blackwell's New York office and the Harvard University Press for providing me with a copy of Freud's recently discovered *Phylogenetic Fantasy* in advance of its publication. Finally, I must thank Alma Gibbons and the LSE computer department for their assistance in preparing the text. To all of these I am most deeply indebted.

Christopher Badcock
August 1987

1

The Fundamental Concept

The Einstein of the mind

Some years ago I was on my way to the Freud house in London when I caught sight of a bizarre spectacle. Outside a nearby library, placed there in honour of the founder of psychoanalysis, was a life-size bronze statue of Freud. But around the head of the statue someone had wound a large black plastic rubbish bag. The effect was stiking to say the least, and looked for all the world like some surreal work of art, particularly considering whose head it was that had been so carefully shrouded from public view.

The library in question was, as it happened, the place where, years earlier still, I initially encountered the works of Freud. On that occasion I was casually browsing when I came across the first volume of his collected works. It appeared to be mainly correspondence, written to someone whose name .I had never heard. But, before long, I was engrossed. Indeed, so engrossed was I that I went on to read the remaining 22 volumes of Freud's writings, more or less in the order in which they were written. Later I was to meet a leading Freudian analyst who maintained that this was the only authentic way to approach Freud's ideas and writings. But reading the complete works in sequence is an undertaking which few will wish to begin and fewer still complete.

Yet interest in Freud and his ideas has never been greater.

Freud, like Einstein, is a name which everybody knows. But psychoanalysis, Freud's new science of the mind, is, like Einstein's relativity, widely misunderstood. This is paradoxical in view of Freud's immense influence on twentieth-century thought, culture and psychological medicine. The insights he has given us into the workings of the mind have brought relief to countless distressed individuals and his science of psychoanalysis employment, professional standing and wide influence to many thousands of counsellors and psychotherapists – some of them orthodox Freudians, many more using methods only peripherally related to psychoanalysis, but all derived, in one way or another, from his pioneering example.

More than this, Freud has changed once and for all our whole manner of looking at ourselves, our relations with others and our conceptions of culture, society and behaviour. He has been described, rightly or wrongly, as the father of feminism; a revolutionary thinker on a par with Karl Marx; a social and sexual reactionary; a moralist who substituted personal fulfilment through psychotherapy for morality based on guilt; an ideologist who undermined the Protestant ethic of duty and hard work; an old-fashioned believer in positive science; a new kind of novelist; a psychologist of genius; a crank; a case of psychopathology, drug-addiction, sexual perversion, and so on, practically *ad infinitum*.

Of course, most of these labels have to be wrong; they cannot possibly all be right. In fact, plain ignorance and misunderstanding of Freud are widespread. For instance, I recently came across a review of something by Freud in a British Sunday newspaper which had been written by a well-known and widely respected literary and academic figure. He began by castigating Freud for writing not factual science but imaginative fiction and cited the case history of Anna O. as an example. As we shall see in the next chapter, Anna O. was actually someone called Bertha Pappenheim and was never treated by Freud, but by one of his early associates, who wrote the case up in a manner which reveals an approach fundamentally different from Freud's. In short, a bigger blunder could hardly be imagined on the part of the reviewer in question whose talent for writing fiction seems more apparent than Freud's. Yet ignorance, prejudice and misunderstanding are all too common where Freud and psychoanalysis is concerned.

The plastic-shrouded statue I had come across had been originally unveiled by the person I was going to visit on that occasion, Freud's heir and successor in psychoanalysis, his youngest daughter Anna Freud (1895–1982); and I immediately climbed up and removed the offending object. The incident seems symbolic of the fate of Freud and evidently seemed so to Anna Freud who, on another occasion but apropos the same subject, once said to me, 'The Freud people see today is not the man I knew; now there are so many myths and misunderstandings.' I would like to think that incident might also be symbolic of this book, intended as it is to reveal the true face of Freud and the essentials of his new science of psychoanalysis.

Sigmund Freud was born (as it happens in a caul, which seems appropriate in the light of the foregoing) on 6 May 1856 in Freiberg, then a town in the Austro-Hungarian province of Moravia (now Příbor in Czechoslovakia). The fact that he died on 23 September 1939 in London shows that, despite his prominence in the twentieth century, slightly more of his life was actually spent in the nineteenth.

Albert Einstein was born in the German city of Ulm in 1879; his father, like Freud's, was a Jewish businessman of moderate means whose family was obliged to migrate with him when business interests dictated it – Freud's family to Vienna in 1860 (when Sigmund was four) and Einstein's to Munich within a year of his birth and later to Milan in 1894 (when Albert was fifteen). Despite the 23-year age-gap that divided the two both men began to publish their revolutionary ideas in the first years of the twentieth century (Einstein's first paper on relativity and Freud's *Three Essays on the Theory of Sexuality* were published in 1905) and both achieved their first widespread fame – or notoriety – after World War I.

The fact that both were Jewish is probably not without significance. Jews had been emancipated in central Europe only in the mid-nineteenth century and Freud and Einstein were part of a great wave of Jewish scientists, intellectuals and artists who were to burst upon the scene of Western culture once their traditional disqualifications were removed. It is almost as if the newly emancipated Jews of central Europe were out to show just what they could do, and to revolutionize the arts and sciences in the process. Among the revolutions which they were to bring about none was to be more significant or to affect later generations more profoundly than relativity or psychoanalysis.

In particular, the development of nuclear weapons and the so-called 'permissive society' might be laid at the door of Einstein and Freud respectively. But even though each would have good grounds for rejecting more than partial responsibility for his particular contribution to those contentious developments, both would have to accept widespread, if indirect and more informal, influence on twentieth-century life. In terms of fundamental ideas related to space, time and motion, Einstein brought about a conceptual revolution every bit as profound and significant as Freud's rethinking of the nature of consciousness, motivation and feeling.

In our perhaps complacent belief in what we think we already know we often overlook an important truth about new scientific insights: the fact that they are usually controversial and nearly always contradict the judgement of common-sense. Take Copernicus's insight about the structure of the solar system as an example. What could be more profoundly counter to common-sense than the assertion that the Earth moves around the sun? Do we feel it moving? We certainly *can* see the sun move – it crosses the sky with a perceptible motion.

Much the same can be said about most scientific advances; and this immediately explains why it is the norm, rather than the exception, for new scientific insights to be greeted with opposition and disbelief on the part of many, rather than immediate acceptance. New scientific insights are nearly always controversial and often seem perversely wrong in the eyes of those who are first confronted with them. In the cases of Freud and Einstein this is unmistakably so, and hardly surprising. What would be most surprising – and a sure indication that something somewhere was fundamentally wrong – would have been a situation in which the fundamental insights of either man had been immediately or easily accepted. That they were not derives not merely from the fact that they were strikingly original and countered what we take to be common-sense, but that they apply to regions of experience with which we are not usually familiar.

In the case of psychoanalysis the difficulty lies in the fact that it, like relativity, is concerned with realities not normally perceptible in everyday life. This is because psychoanalysis takes a fundamentally different view of human psychology to that which dominates our subjective, day-to-day awareness of it. Furthermore, such a subjective, common-sense view has also been responsible for the attitude taken by philosophers and by academic psychologists who, exactly like philosophers and physicists before Einstein, have preferred the obvious, apparent reality to that revealed by twentieth-century science.

Mental topography

Just as philosophers before Einstein assumed that space and time were ultimate categories of reason rather than the perplexing physical realities which relativity showed them to be, so Freud revealed that the normal, 'obvious', philosophical meaning of the term 'consciousness' could not be what had been supposed. For the philosophers, consciousness was exactly what space and time were before relativity: rational categories, concepts which they believed to be more or less identical with rational thought itself. Yet just as Einstein took his first momentous stride towards relativity by side-stepping such subjective suppositions and instead defined time as that which was measured by clocks and space as what was indicated by measuring-rods, so Freud redefined *consciousness* as *whatever is actually conscious at any given moment*. Using his own words, 'let us call "conscious" the conception which is present to our consciousness and of which we are aware, and let this be the only meaning of the term "conscious".'*

Admittedly, this is a category, but it is not an all-inclusive one; furthermore, it is defined by reference to psychological reality, not subjective prejudice or philosophical argument. It does not include that of which I am unaware at this moment, but might be aware in the next, or was aware in the past. It is not an undivided field of awareness like that envisaged by philosophers or suggested by our everyday attitude. By comparison with the latter, Freud's more accurately defined consciousness is a very limited thing, restricted to the immediately and really conscious. Furthermore, like Einstein's concepts of space and time, Freud's concept of consciousness is defined by a perceptible reality, not a philosopher's assumption.

This immediately raises the problem of what to do with all the rest that the philosophers might have wanted to include in their broad categorization of consciousness. An example might be my telephone number, of which I am not conscious until I allude to it; or, to take another, the position of a letter on a typewriter key-board, which is immediately known by my fingers but which my conscious mind can take some time to locate. Such potentially

preconscious

*'A Note on the Unconscious in Psychoanalysis', *The Standard Edition of the Complete Psychological Works of Sigmund Freud* (London, 1953–1974), vol. XII, p. 260.

conscious things as these Freud termed *pre-conscious*; he meant, by that term, whatever might become conscious, but is not directly subject to conscious awareness at any one moment.

Yet here again we must notice an important difference between Freud's approach and that of the philosophers, one which my second example will illustrate. This is the fact that Freud's view of consciousness is both *topographical* and *dynamic*, rather than merely categorical and descriptive.

If the entire contents of the mind could be conscious in exactly the same way, then the broadly categorizing approach of the philosophers might be justified. They would be giving the same name to the same thing, which is perfectly legitimate. But my example of finding a letter on a key-board shows that this is not so. Suppose I want to locate the letter 'z' in the alphabet: I find it immediately because I know that it is the last and is preceded by 'x' and 'y'. Although Freud would call my consiousness of the positions of these letters pre-conscious until I actually thought of them – when they would become conscious in his sense of the word – a philosopher might object that this was just cheese-paring – something of which philosophers are usually accused, not psychoanalysts!

Yet let us compare this with the situation which occurs if I am asked to think consciously of the position of 'z' on a key-board. I immediately find that this is not quite so easy. My fingers seem to know 'instinctively' where to find it, but my conscious mind has to hunt around; and saying which letters are immediately adjacent to it seems an almost impossible task, at least when compared with the alphabet, which I know easily.

But I also 'know' where 'z' is because when typing at speed my fingers find it just as easily as any other letter. It seems that what has happened is that my knowledge of where 'z' is located on the key-board of a typewriter has become almost completely *unconscious* mainly because I have learnt its location in terms of manipulation, rather than by conscious reference to a map of the key-board. This means that when I am typing – as I am at this instant – I do not have any conscious realization of exactly what my fingers are doing when they type 'z'. On the contrary, my consciousness is preoccupied with what I am typing in *verbal* terms, the typography I am content to leave to an apparently automatic, 'instinctive' knowledge which does not concern my immediate conscious awareness. Yet such knowledge cannot be genuinely instinctive because I had to learn it. We are forced to conclude that what must have begun as a fully conscious awareness of the location of 'z' when I was learning to type has now become a more or less completely unconscious knowledge which I can use without directly rehearsing it as a conscious picture of the key-board comparable to my conscious knowledge of the ordering of the alphabet.

The point of this demonstration is to illustrate what is certainly one of the essential characteristics of Freudian psychology: namely, that its approach to consciousness and to mental events in general is topographical. In the example above a piece of knowledge starts out as fully conscious in the Freudian sense, so that when I was learning to type I had consciously to picture the location of 'z' on the key-board. But by dint of repeated practice I found that this piece of conscious knowledge gradually became rooted in the pre-conscious and, what is more, in a manner in which its recall is almost impossible without either searching a particular key-board or locating it by actually typing. The fact that it is much more difficult to recall than its position in the alphabet illustrates the fundamental point: consciousness is not homogeneous and undivided. On the contrary, it is highly subdivided, convoluted and compartmentalized; in psychoanalytic terms, it manifests a topography: that is, different levels or localities where mental events occur in various ways, dependent on their relative positions.

Psychological dynamics

The consequence of this way of looking at things is that an entire spectrum of states exists with regard to ·so-called 'consciousness', ranging from complete, immediate and self-conscious awareness to complete unconsciousness, with everything in between. On this continuum it seems that my knowledge of the position of 'z' in the alphabet is somewhat nearer the surface of complete consciousness than is my knowledge of its key-board position. Furthermore, if we take my difficulty in recalling its position in the key-board situation seriously then we might envisage something which makes the Freudian approach manifestly different from that of the philosophers, or of pre-Freudian common sense. We might conceive the possibility – clearly implied in what was argued above – that some mental events might become totally unconscious to the extent that the topographical view would predispose us to conceive of a third compart-mentalization of consciousness, one beyond the reach of consciousness altogether, not pre-conscious, but wholly *unconscious*.

Here, once again, the typewriter suggests an illustration. Some years ago I was busy at work on the manuscript of a book one Saturday morning. Since this was the Saturday of a Bank Holiday weekend (that is one which, for the benefit of readers abroad, repeats the abomination known as the British Sunday the following Monday), my wife asked me when I was going to stop writing and devote some time to the family. Telling her that I would do so later, but was not going to let such a long period of leisure pass without devoting quite a lot of it to my work, I continued typing.

Some 15 or 20 minutes later my typewriter suddenly broke down – or so it seemed. The ribbon-feed, responsible for advancing and raising the ribbon in front of the type, appeared to have malfunctioned. No amount of fiddling about – not even fitting a new ribbon – seemed to avail. I cursed my luck and set off for the typewriter repair shop in the town, only to find it closed because of the Bank Holiday. Frustrated by the perverse working of fate, I announced to my family that I was now completely free for the duration, to my wife's evident approval.

The holiday passed. On the Bank Holiday Monday evening, not long before going to bed, I was sitting talking to my wife about nothing in particular – certainly, about nothing to do with my writing – when an idea suddenly 'popped' into my mind. I use this expression advisedly because this is how it seemed. An apparently ready-made idea appeared complete and unrehearsed in my consciousness. I rushed up to my typewriter and immediately saw that I was right. A small lever in the upper right-hand corner of the key-board could be set to stop the ribbon-feed (for purposes of cutting stencils) between two other settings corresponding to the black or red side of the ribbon. Somehow or other I had inadvertently moved this lever to the mid-way position, and immediately I moved it back all was well with the typewriter. Had I known, I could have done that before, when the apparent fault first occurred. I could, after all, have worked over the weekend!

To many readers this may seem to be an unremarkable event, annoying, but without any further significance. Yet I was not so sure. One or two things about it perplexed me. For instance, why did I only recall the possibility that the ribbon-feed control might have been moved as the Bank Holiday period was ending, and not before, when my concern with it was greatest? If that possibility had been lodged in my pre-conscious like my telephone number why could I not recall it when I needed it most? Again, how had I come to move the lever in the first place? For the fact is that never in many years use had such a thing occurred, and it never happened again. Indeed, when I attempted to reconstruct the accidental movement of that tiny lever I found it almost impossible. A careless fumble in its direction – itself inexplicable since it was away from all the other typographical keys – would only produce a complete movement from the 'black' to 'red' position; it seemed almost impossible to knock it accidentally into the intermediate one.

Consequently, I began to consider a different explanation. Rather than just explain it away as an accident, it occurred to me that it might in fact have been motivated. We will recall that I was in a state of some minor, but real inner conflict: my wife wanted me to leave my typing, I wanted to continue. On both sides the motives were significant. On the one side was my love for my wife and my desire to please her and to be seen to be an adequate and responsive husband and father. On the other, that unrelenting pressure to publish which anyone in university circles will recognize only too well. Here my professional responsibilities and ambitions came into direct, if temporary, conflict with those relating to my family. I tried to avoid the conflict by insisting that I must continue to work; but the suppressed alternative to this, the desire to do what my wife – and, evidently, an important part of myself – wanted, found a way of expressing itself by what I can only regard as a classical Freudian slip.

Without consciously noticing it I somehow sabotaged my own conscious intention and put my typewriter into a state in which I could not continue typing. But this could only be achieved if my knowledge of what must have happened was somehow kept unconscious. However – and I regard this as the real give-away of the whole thing – once the Bank Holiday period was nearly over the occasion for the whole conflict ebbed away and with it the need to maintain my ignorance of the true cause of the trouble with the typewriter. This explains why on the Monday evening my pre-conscious knowledge of the possibility of manipulating the ribbon-feed lever in the way in which I evidently did suddenly returned to consciousness as a complete and pre-formed realization.

I had known it all along; but not as the philosophers

might have said I knew it, not as a permanent, static piece of knowledge like something written in a book which I could recall at will as if it were my telephone number or some other item of pre-conscious knowledge. On the contrary, during that weekend I had known it *unconsciously*. My ignorance of it resulted from the fact that the topography of consciousness is a direct result of Freud's fundamental insight: the realization that most important mental events are *dynamic* and the outcome of opposing forces, ideas and wishes. According to the dynamic view, conflict, movement and variation dominate mental life, rather than some static, fixed or unchanging condition.

To put the matter another way, we might conclude that I had a *resistance* to knowing what had really happened to my typewriter because, by not knowing about it, I had spared myself the consciousness of some mental conflict and the resultant anguish which such conflict brings. My response had been a characteristically defensive one to a typically dynamic conflict. Unconsciously I had made my typewriter make up my mind for me and present me with a situation in which I could quite legitimately – or, so it seemed – forget the whole conflict between my professional and family commitments.

In this instance resistance shows itself as a desire to avoid pain and anguish by appearing to solve a conflict between contradictory desires, each legitimate in its own way but quite incompatible as far as its realization was concerned. In a similar way, Freud was to see science as encountering resistance – resistance motivated by a comparable situation: the desire to avoid an unpleasant conflict between contradictory wishes.

Repression, pleasure principle and reality

The concept of resistance, at least as it is understood by psychoanalysis, may seem a somewhat controversial idea.

Some, perhaps more interested in appearing to make clever criticisms than to understand it, have depicted it as a kind of 'Catch-22' tactic by means of which the analyst is right if you agree but also right if you do not – the latter instance reflecting so-called 'resistance'.

In reality, there is nothing particularly controversial about the concept of resistance. What it means is that the analyst treats denials rather as they are treated in a court of law, where it is normally assumed that a confession is true but a denial may or may not be. In practice, resistances usually advertise themselves by their stridency. Someone who starts denying or affirming something with much more passion than the matter deserves is usually doing so for some very good reason – something as true in everyday life as it is in the analyst's consulting room. An example might be the analytic rule-of-thumb which says that if someone gives one reason for something it is probably fair enough, but several reasons should arouse suspicion. This is based on the sound psychological principle that no one needs more than one good reason for doing anything; more begin to look like excuses or justifications and naturally invite further scrutiny.

As applied to science, the idea of resistance is found in the works of a great French astronomer, the Marquis de Laplace. He argued that opposition to the realization that the Earth was not the centre of the universe originated not only in the 'illusions of the senses', but in the 'self-love' of mankind. In other words, we resisted the idea that the sun rather than the Earth was the centre of the solar system because it affronted human pride to suggest that our world was not the focus of creation.*

In Freud's view this was only the first of three great challenges which science made to what he – evidently echoing Laplace – called 'the naive self-love of men'. The second, perhaps even more devastating blow, was dealt by Darwin's theory of evolution. No longer the centre of the

*Pierre Simon, Marquis de Laplace, *System of the World*, (Paris, 1799), Part 1, ch. 6.

universe, we now discovered that even in the biological world our position was in no way special or central. On the contrary, we were the product of blind evolutionary forces just like any other species and shared a common ancestor with those most comical of all creatures, the apes. Finally, Freud suggested that a third great challenge to our vanity and pretentiousness might be seen coming from psychoanalysis when it showed that consciousness was not even master in its own house but that, on the contrary, an extensive unconscious existed which could on occasions have far-reaching effects on behaviour, thought and feeling.*

My earlier example of the mysteriously sabotaged typewriter is an instance of such an effect. Yet even in this trivial instance I experienced a distinct shock to my feelings about myself. I was forced to admit that I was capable of doing things I had no conscious recollection of doing; and, furthermore, that my knowledge of what I had done seemed to be kept from me for as long as it was important that I be kept in ignorance. At best this produced an uncanny feeling; at worst a real affront to my mental self-possession. However one looks at it, it is an unpleasant thing to have to admit that one can act under the influence of an unconscious compulsion and that one's knowledge of one's own mind is, on occasions at least, severely curtailed.

One inevitable consequence of this is that psychoanalytic insights, like other scientific truths, but much more so, encounter fierce resistance. Here, 'resistan e' can be understood in a colloquial sense: psychoanalysis is controversial; but it can also be understood in a more technical sense, namely, as a special case of *repression*.

Of all Freudian concepts, few are more fundamentally and routinely misunderstood than the mechanism of repression, which can claim to be absolutely central to psychoanalysis. For our present purposes, it might be best to approach its true Freudian meaning by returning to our

*S. Freud, *Introductory Lectures on Psychoanalysis, Standard Edition*, vol. XVI pp. 284–5.

previous consideration of the nature of consciousness.

If consciousness is topographical in the technical sense explained above (that is, subdivided into different levels or regions), we need to ask ourselves what brings this differentiation into existence. What is it that makes some things conscious, some pre-conscious and some totally unconscious?

The factor which distinguishes conscious from pre-conscious seems mainly to be the nature of attention, which, if directed at one thing, cannot normally be directed at another. The fact that I cannot normally recall the exact key-board location of the 'z' key whereas I can that of its alphabetical position suggests that something has intervened to erase, suppress or at least weaken its representation in consciousness. Presumably the explanation is that knowledge of its position has become part of a motor-skill which can function reliably without conscious attention.

In the case of the typewriter breakdown the mechanism seems to be clear. A piece of pre-conscious knowledge (the possibility of moving the ribbon-feed lever) suddenly threatened my mental equilibrium – if I had remembered it on the Saturday morning when the incident occurred I would have been left facing the dilemma of either obeying my wish to satisfy my obligation to my family or ignoring it and going on with my work. Disconcertingly, something in me changed the status of that piece of knowledge so that it ceased to be in the pre-conscious region of my mind (in other words, accessible to conscious realization) and instead became, temporarily at least, completely *unconscious*.

In short, I had forgotten it. Such forgetting, along with the forgetting that we have forgotten, is the essence of repression; in Freud's own words, '*repression lies simply in turning something away, and keeping it at a distance from consciousness.*'*

From a dynamic point of view (that is, one which sees

---

*'Repression', *Standard Edition*, vol. XIV, p. 147; Freud's emphasis.

mental events in terms of the conflict of opposing forces), repression is an active force which attempts to change mental topography by forcing certain of the contents of the conscious or the pre-conscious into the unconscious and then does its best to keep them there. I say 'attempts' and 'does its best' advisedly because, as my example suggests and as the findings of psychoanalysis clearly show, repression is a far from efficient mechanism. It seems that it could keep my knowledge of what had happened to my typewriter out of consciousness for as long as the conflict which had occasioned the original repression lasted, but once that began to pass off with the ending of the holiday period repression relented and the repressed returned.

However, since repression is a dynamic psychological factor its activities are not restricted to single instances like this one. If we take the dynamic foundation of the topographical view of the conscious seriously we must conclude that mental topography as a whole – the real, active distinction between conscious, pre-conscious and unconscious – is maintained by the force of repression and that this, in its turn, exists to attempt to safeguard consciousness from conflict, anxiety and contradiction. Resistance to psychological insights such as the concept of repression itself is only another aspect of this more general principle of mental dynamics.

In this sense such repressions serve the interests of what Freud called the *pleasure principle*. By this he meant an innate tendency to want to maximize pleasure and minimize pain. To see repression described as serving the pleasure principle may surprise many readers who may be used to habitually thinking of repression in non-Freudian terms. However, I have expressed the matter in this way intentionally because I wanted to bring out as clearly as possible the contrast between the technical, psychoanalytic meaning of repression and the colloquial, everyday use. This is an important matter since the misunderstanding and misuse of this term has contributed to much confusion about what Freud really meant. To quote his own words: 'There is no doubt that the resistance of the conscious and unconscious ego operates under the sway of the pleasure principle: it seeks to avoid the unpleasure which would be produced by the liberation of the repressed.'*

The everyday use of 'repression' may lead to its confusion with what, from Freud's view, is almost the exact opposite: namely, conscious repudiation or *suppression*. In my example above we saw that I consciously repudiated my wife's advice – I went on working, and intended to do so over the weekend. Yet this resulted in a repression appearing which expressed itself as an inability to recall something I usually knew – how to stop the ribbon-feed (along with another one which almost certainly made me not notice moving the lever in the first place). These repressions were wholly unconscious. I did not know that I had 'accidentally' done something and then forgotten how to undo it. I did know that I had rejected my wife's admonitions. The latter was a conscious repudiation of a wish dictated by reality; the former an unconscious gratification of a counter-wish more concerned with avoiding pain and internal conflict than meeting the demands of the real world.

Contrary to the common misapprehension of what repression means in psychoanalysis, it cannot be seen as standing in place of a gratification of a pleasure – after all, why should it? Gratifications are, by definition, gratifying, and so one would hardly want to repress them. In the quotation earlier Freud remarked that the aim of repression is *to avoid the unpleasure which would be produced by the liberation of the repressed*. In other words, repression stands in place of a painful conflict, not a gratifying pleasure; it aims to escape pain, not to deny gratification as such.

Furthermore, the undoing of a repression cannot be

*S. Freud, *Beyond the Pleasure Principle, Standard Edition*, vol. XVIII, p. 20.

expected to be necessarily gratifying if its whole justification lies in avoiding pain and anguish. On the contrary, it is much more likely to increase conflict and to lead to the reappearance of the original unpleasant feelings which motivated its creation in the first place.

Again, the popular misconception of what repression means tends to equate it with something like political repression, which is carried out by one individual or group against another. But repression in psychoanalysis is quite different. It occurs only within the mind; and only the individual in question can be responsible for it. No one else can carry out a repression for you in the psychoanalytic sense of the term.

In summary, it cannot be stressed too much in drawing attention to the distinctive Freudian meaning of the term *repression* that such repressions are autonomous, unconscious and involuntary, and that the unconscious is consequently an inaccessible region of the mind which obeys the pleasure principle, at least as far as conscious awareness is concerned.

This explains why psychoanalysis, like relativity, seems to relate to strange and surprising realities which we seldom encounter in our everyday, waking consciousness – and which if we do come across them, we usually shrug off as 'accidents', 'mistakes' or 'nonsense'. Yet, just as relativistic effects fall below the level of detectability in most aspects of everyday life but are real nevertheless, so such psychoanalytic realities as repression, although unknown and unseen, nevertheless occur. This is why we cannot dismiss psychoanalytic insights merely by denying conscious knowledge of them. We might like to think that we are always and everywhere conscious of what is in our own minds and what our true motives are, but careful examination of actual behaviour (like my analysis of the typewriter incident) shows unmistakably that this cannot be so. Believing that 'consciousness' and 'the mind' are exactly the same thing leads to a shallow conception of human mental life and to psychology of astonishing triviality.

Furthermore, because mental life and the topography of consciousness are governed by dynamic factors – that is, by conflicts of countervailing forces and wishes – we probably have good reasons of our own for denying that such conflicts exist. If the pleasure principle predicts that human beings want to avoid mental conflict, anguish and discomfort in general, then it follows that a recognition of such conflicts in ourselves will probably involve real anxiety (at the very least, what Freud called *unpleasure* in the quotation earlier). This mental discomfort will be comparable to what motivated my slip with the typewriter: a desire to avoid a clash between incompatible desires, between opposing wishes or conflicting interests. It will show itself as resistance to scientific insights which, like Freud's, seek to bring such mental dynamics to the notice of consciousness and consequently to serve to remind it of all that it is trying to forget – the repressed. Where psychoanalysis is concerned it does not seem unlikely that it is a reluctance to want to experience inner conflict, so fundamental to the structure of consciousness itself, which might tempt us to reject it and turn to something much more pleasurable and reassuring.

Yet the pleasure principle cannot have things all its own way. In order to function at all we must take account of reality and the constraints which it puts on our wishes. For this reason Freud saw consciousness and the perceptual system which feeds it with information about the outside world as dominated by another, opposing factor, what he called the *reality principle*.

Mental life may well be motivated by the desire to avoid pain and to maximize pleasure, but it cannot afford to ignore reality in trying to achieve those ends. Reality, as we know to our cost, can impose some very considerable pain if we ignore it foolishly; and just about every gratification of a wish involves some consideration of reality. The pleasure principle might make me look forward to eating at lunchtime, but reality must enter the picture if I am to find something to eat in the real world where not everything is edible or available to be eaten just when and where my unconscious might wish. In other words, consciousness must take account of reality in its management of its wishes and cannot expect to indulge the pleasure principle without consideration of its additional implications for reality.

Here, inevitably, is a prime cause of conflict and a major factor in mental dynamics. This is because, almost always, repression and resistance will seek to gratify the pleasure principle while consciousness seeks to deal with the frustrations, delays and complications dictated by reality.

Yet the two principles are by no means incompatible. Real gratifications of the pleasure principle can be achieved in the real world – indeed, we might go further and say that, in general, they can *only* by achieved there. The consequence is that they can be reconciled by consciousness, largely thanks to the realization that the legitimate demands of the pleasure principle are a part of reality and should be treated by consciousness accordingly. Wanting to have my lunch may well be a wish dictated by the pleasure principle but the reality principle also dictates that I gratify it in some way if I wish to maintain my physical well-being.

It is here perhaps more than anywhere else that psychoanalysis finds its ultimate justification: as a realization on the part of consciousness of the true nature of its constitution and of the reality surrounding itself – not merely the external reality accessible to the perceptual system, but the internal reality of which it is a part. Furthermore, such self-knowledge is not merely desirable as an ideal; it is essential if we are to avoid the cost which ignoring it entails.

The cost in question is a limitation of consciousness and a misunderstanding of what is actually occurring in our own minds. Self-deception may well gratify the pleasure principle in the short run, but it can have disastrous consequences for our adaptation to reality in the longer term. Denying the value of insight into the dynamic unconscious may well correspond, metaphorically speaking, not so much to shrouding the face of Freud as to blinkering ourselves to the reality which is within us. In this respect Freud is as much of a challenge to our moral courage as he is to our intellect. Ultimately, psychoanalysis may be much more than the dynamic psychology of mental topography; it may be a crucial test of how much truth we can tolerate about ourselves.

2

The First Psychoanalytic Revolution

Hypnosis and hysteria

If one had to put a date to the beginning of 'the psychoanalytic revolution' the year 1900 might seem natural, marking as it does the publication date of Freud's *Interpretation of Dreams*, as well as a new century. But another strong candidate might be 1895, the year in which Freud, along with his associate Joseph Breuer (1842–1925), published *Studies on Hysteria*.

In this remarkable book Breuer recorded the case history of his patient referred to throughout as 'Anna O.', but now known to have been Bertha Pappenheim (1859–1936). At the time she fell ill in 1880 Bertha was 21 years old. According to Breuer she 'possessed a powerful intellect' and had 'great poetic and imaginative gifts.'*

During and following the illness and death of her much-loved father, Bertha developed alarming hysterical symptoms. Disturbances of vision and balance, seizures and loss of sensation in various limbs, nervous cough, inability to eat and drink, trance-like states, headache and other things appeared along with terrifying hallucinations of snakes in her hair, death's heads and skeletons. At times she showed

*All the references here are from *Studies on Hysteria, Standard Edition of the Complete Psychological Works of Sigmund Freud* (London, 1953–1974), vol. II.

evidence of two quite distinct states of consciousness: a relatively normal one and another, hallucinatory one in which she was abusive and violent towards herself and others. She complained of an inability to think and of laborious 'recognizing work' when she met people. Her speech became disorganized so that at times she only spoke in telegraphic style; at other times only in English or other languages, affecting not to understand German when it was spoken to her. Although able to read French and Italian, if asked to do so out loud 'she produced, with extraordinary fluency. . .an admirable extempore English translation.' When first introduced to Freud by Breuer she was initially unable to see him, manifesting a so-called 'negative hallucination'; but then fell unconscious when he made his presence felt by gently blowing cigar smoke in her face.

. Breuer's first report of this case seems to have had little initial impact on Freud. Following his secondary education, Freud had enrolled as a medical student at the University of Vienna, taking many years over his studies and doing valuable research into cell physiology in the laboratory of Ernst von Brücke (1819–1892) – a leading member of the Helmholtz school of thought which held that all biological phenomena have a purely physical basis. In his histological researches Freud showed great capacity for painstaking observation and description, but – rather like Einstein – little aptitude for experimental studies.

Following graduation, and choosing neurology as a speciality (and narrowly missing achieving world fame by his work on cocaine in 1884), Freud obtained a grant to travel to Paris to study under Jean-Martin Charcot (1825–1893).

By contrast to the anti-psychological, Viennese school led by Theodor Meynert (1833–1892) which claimed that hysteria had a purely physical basis, Charcot's demonstrations showed that suggestion – a psychological factor – also played a part. He illustrated this fact to great effect at his famous Tuesday lectures to which, along with foreign visitors like Freud, the cream of Parisian intellectual society evidently also came, drawn as much by the bizarre and theatrical behaviour of the hysterics put on show there as by the standing of Charcot himself, who was sometimes called the Napoleon of the Neuroses.

By demonstrating that symptoms indistinguishable from 'genuine' hysteria could be induced in hypnotic subjects who lacked such symptoms in waking life, Charcot appeared to have shown that a *mental* factor underlay them. For instance, a favourite demonstration of his was to substitute symptoms. Two hysterics would be brought on, one, shall we say, suffering from a paralysis of the right leg, the other from loss of sensation in the left arm. Under hypnosis Charcot would demonstrate that now the patient with the leg problem had lost sensation in the arm and that the other patient could not move the right leg!

The contention that hysterical symptoms were psychological, rather than physiological, in origin was further corroborated by the fact that typical hysterical afflictions ignored the laws of neurophysiology and principles of anatomy in order to obey the preconceptions of the patients. It was found that it was not so much the neurology of the limb or area of the body which was involved in a hysterical disturbance as the patient's perception of it. All this suggested that psychology rather than physiology was implicated in such cases.

Inevitably, Freud's espousal of Charcot's theories and his use of hypnotism made him unpopular in Vienna. There, the orthodox view taught that it was purely physical factors like blood supply to the brain which caused hysterical symptoms. It is important to recall that suggestion was by no means as widely accepted as it is today and to remember that, in the last quarter of the nineteenth century, hypnosis was usually regarded as a sham – 'play-acting' – something suitable for the theatre (where those under the hypnotic influence were often said to be in collusion with the hypnotist) rather than medical science. The 'animal magnetism' of Mesmer was so much mysticism, the whole subject of hypnotism was thoroughly disreputable.

Yet, on his return to Vienna from his visit to Paris in 1886, Freud did find one or two others who were prepared to believe that there might be something in hypnotism and that hysterical symptoms might have psychological – as opposed to purely physical – causes. Chief among these was Breuer, like himself a Jewish physician, and some 14 years his senior.

Following a further trip to France, this time to perfect his technique with the celebrated hypnotherapists Hippolyte Bernheim (1837–1919) and Auguste Liébeault (1823–1904) at Nancy, Freud began to take a real interest in Breuer's Bertha. It seems that, having previously brought the case to the attention of the Napoleon of the Neuroses, but having failed to interest him in it, the Einstein of the mind also forget about it, at least temporarily. But back in Vienna in the early 1890s both Freud and Breuer resolved to try to provide a psychological explanation of hysterias like that afflicting Bertha Pappenheim. *Studies on Hysteria* (1895) was the result of their collaboration.

Although it was Freud, and not Breuer, who visited Charcot and the Nancy hypnotists, Breuer's interpretation of Bertha's illness stayed closer to the assumptions of the French school of thought. Even though Breuer commented on the fact that she was '*completely unsuggestible*' and spoke of Bertha's pronounced 'obstinacy' and powerful intellect, he nevertheless believed that her symptoms were induced by suggestion, much as Charcot had induced such symptoms during his famous demonstrations. The only difference was that, according to Breuer's theory, it was a question of *auto-suggestion* produced in what he termed a *hypnoid state*.

According to Breuer's theory, during suitable periods of mental vacancy induced by the lengthy nursing of her dying father, Bertha had lapsed into a self-induced state of hypnosis during which her notable tendency to indulge in day-dreaming and fantasy began to get the better of her, causing her to suggest to herself various morbid ideas which then conditioned her symptoms and the course of her illness. In Breuer's view she was a hypnotic subject who had become her own hypnotist, a patient who demonstrated Charcot's ideas without the intervention of the great man himself.

Bertha herself termed these hypnoid states 'clouds' – a period of somnolence which regularly occurred in the evenings. Breuer had come to the conclusion that she was oppressed by things which she could not bring herself to talk about. However, if, following 'clouds', she could be induced to recount her hallucinations and feelings, 'she would wake up clear in mind, calm and cheerful.' Bertha called this 'the talking cure' and the process involved she graphically termed 'chimney-sweeping'. Essentially it was what Freud and Breuer called the *cathartic method*: a form of psychotherapy by means of which hysterics were induced to unburden their minds of whatever it was that was afflicting them and thereby gain relief from their symptoms.

An amusing anecdote once told me by an acquaintance nicely illustrates the fundamental principle. The man in question had been brought up in a strict religious household and drafted into the Royal Navy during World War II. There he was continually exposed to torrents of bad language of the kind he had never heard at home, let alone been allowed to use himself. So disturbing was all this that he found that it kept him awake at night and that the only way he could get to sleep was to lie in bed repeating under his breath each and every swear-word, oath and obscenity he had heard that day!

This continued for some time. Then one day he accidently dropped a heavy naval shell on his toes and could not hold back a verbal protest entirely in keeping with naval tradition. From that moment onwards he was cured of his insomnia and never again had to resort to his bed-time litany of swearing. Evidently, day-time expression had cured him of it.

In a comparable way, Freud and Breuer believed that

Bertha had bottled up inside herself something which had to be allowed to drain off in her verbal reports, evidently to her marked relief. They assumed that it was because she could not otherwise express this material that she was subject to the symptoms of her illness. In his case history Breuer reports that, following a break in the treatment, he found that he had to relieve 'her of the whole stock of imaginative products which she had accumulated since my last visit'. 'She knew that after she had given utterance to her hallucinations she would lose all her obstinacy and what she described as her "energy".'

Freud and Breuer called this process of recollection and expression *abreaction* and for them it represented the therapeutic equivalent of the release of bottled-up feelings and expression brought about in my anecdote about my naval acquaintance when the shell fell on his foot. Essentially, the cathartic method of psychotherapy aimed to achieve a comparable release of inner tension through the influence of the therapist.

Bertha's mention of 'losing her energy' during the process of abreaction suggests a further dimension to our discussion of the mind outlined in the previous chapter. It suggests that, along with the topographical and dynamic accounts, we must add a *quantitative* (or 'economic') one as well. It is not just that Bertha was upset by contradictory feelings engendered by her father's illness and death, or that something of an active, dynamic nature made her wish to forget it – resulting in the 'obstinacy', or resistance mentioned by Breuer above – but that a definite quantity of some kind of nervous energy sought an outlet. The fact that allowing her to verbalize her feelings and fantasies freely resulted in an improvement in her condition and a reduction in her symptoms suggested that the symptoms, and perhaps the entire disorder, were fed by this dammed-up 'energy'.

It was this quantitative factor that was eventually to lead to a split between Freud and Breuer and to take Freud beyond the cathartic method to psychoanalysis proper. To

understand how this came about we need to look closely at
the differences in interpretation between the two authors of
Studies on Hysteria.

Trauma and the pressure method

As we have seen, Breuer interpreted Bertha's hysteria in
terms of auto-suggestion. He related the ease with which
she fell into a 'hypnoid state' to two general and one specific
predisposing factors. The general factors were her monot-
onous family life and habit of day-dreaming; and the one
specific condition the fact that, while nursing her father, she
had to stay awake at night, but tended to sleep in the early
evening. He could agree with Freud that, in a memorable
phrase from their joint introduction to *Studies on Hysteria*, 'hysterics suffer mainly from reminiscences'. But reminiscences
of what?

Breuer gives an instance: Bertha's inability to drink any
kind of liquid. Here the reminiscence turned out to be that
of having seen a dog drinking from a glass, one which,
when 'talked away', ceased to bother her any further.
Again, her hysterical paralyses seemed to originate from a
waking dream – that is, one dreamt in a hypnoid state –
when, sitting at her father's bedside she had seen a black
snake which she tried to fend off. Breuer agreed that in
Bertha's case most of the symptoms seemed to originate in
frights, but he differed from Freud in emphasizing static
factors, such as the predisposing conditions and the mental
state of the patient at the time the symptoms first occurred.

Breuer accepted that within Bertha one could differentiate
two distinct states of consciousness and in fact used the term
'unconscious' in the psychoanalytic sense for the first time
in his discussion of the case. But he restricted the dynamic,
topographical view to hysterics and held that auto-
suggestion 'created the space or region of unconscious
psychological activity into which the ideas which are fended

off are driven'. Unlike Freud, who regarded the unconscious as the product of a dynamic force of repression as likely to be found in normal people as in hysterics, Breuer saw mental topography as resulting from a static condition: the hypnoid state which created the conditions for autosuggestion seen in Bertha.

According to Breuer's way of looking at it, almost any reminiscence might produce a symptom if the conditions were right – even an apparently innocuous scene such as a dog drinking from a glass. If it was a pathological kind of self-hypnosis which was the cause of symptoms, then in principle any kind of idea could lead to a hysteria. What seemed critical was not the experience itself so much as the conditions under which it occurred.

By contrast to this view, Freud's was much more dynamic; and a number of other factors predisposed him to go somewhat beyond Breuer's interpretation. In the first place, Freud had many more patients to treat than did his colleague and found that he simply could not induce hypnotic trance in all of them. Almost certainly, the reason for this was the type of client he treated. By contrast to the Nancy hypnotherapists, who seemed to enjoy a greater percentage of successes where hypnosis was concerned, Freud's clientele was not predominantly working-class. Probably the almost superstitious reverence from patients who were their social inferiors contributed to Liébeault and Bernheim's hypnotic authority over them. Freud enjoyed no such advantage. His clients were more on a par with himself in social standing, were sophisticated citizens of a metropolis and were, in any case, consulting a man whose reputation was at best slight and certainly not comparable to that of the luminaries of the Nancy school. Consequently, it is not surprising that Freud had problems in inducing hypnotic sleep. Much more important, he found an ingenious way round it, one suggested to him, interestingly enough, by Liébeault.

The latter had shown Freud something which was to be

as momentous as the demonstrations of Charcot: this was that a subject could be made to recall apparently unconscious memories of what had taken place in a hypnotic trance if commanded to do so, especially if assisted by gentle pressure of the therapist's hand on the subject's forehead. Gradually Freud abandoned hypnosis for this aptly named *pressure method.*

Patients were asked to concentrate by shutting their eyes and reclining on a comfortable couch. Freud's dynamic approach to repression led him to believe that the causes of his patients' symptoms could be recovered from the unconscious just as apparently forgotten memories of the hypnotic trance could be recalled. His confidence in this assumption was strengthened by success with the recall of objective facts which could be independently checked, such as dates and numbers. Unlike Breuer, who assumed that hysteria originated in twilight states of self-hypnosis, Freud grasped a much more simple and fundamental idea: 'that before hysteria can be acquired. . .an idea must be *intentionally repressed from consciousness*'. An example might be the case of Lucy R., analysed in the book.

The emergence of the dynamic view

Lucy R. was a governess referred to Freud because she suffered from a loss of the sense of smell, along with persistent subjective sensations of two particular smells: those of burnt pudding and, less often, cigar smoke. Lying on the couch and asked to concentrate on the first occurrence of the predominant smell of burnt pudding, the lady managed to recall a domestic scene which had involved conflict with the other servants in her employer's household, as a result of which she announced an intention to resign (but did not do so). Although not a particularly pleasant memory, this seems hardly the stuff of which hysterical symptoms are made (rather like Bertha's reaction to the dog drinking from the glass). Whereas Breuer might have accepted this at face value and explained it away as a consequence of the patient being in a hypnoid state at the time (despite the fact that there was absolutely no evidence for such a supposition), Freud was more circumspect, and guessed that there must be more to it than that.

Believing that deeper, more powerful feelings must be involved, he suggested that Lucy had in fact been secretly in love with her employer and that the conflict about her presence in the household therefore had a more profound cause. She immediately confirmed this insight, although with the admission that she 'didn't know – or rather. . . didn't want to know' and wanted to 'drive it out of my head and not think about it again', and had believed that she had succeeded. There followed many corroborating details which suggested that she had overcome a major resistance; but still the symptoms lingered.

Freud persisted. It appeared that the first and predominant smell, that of the pudding which had burnt at the time of the first scene, had now vanished and a second, subsidiary smell of cigar smoke had taken its place. He tried the pressure method. Prompted by Freud, Lucy now began to recall a further incident in which her employer had chastised her for allowing the children in her charge to kiss a visitor. This had occurred at the time when her feelings for her employer had first been powerfully aroused and so this unpleasant scene, with its erotic overtones associated with kissing and children, had come as a disastrous blow to her hopes. The later incident with the burnt pudding was only a repetition, a reminder of this earlier and much more upsetting one for which the second, subsidiary smell acted as a symbol.

Following this, the symptoms vanished completely and what had remained a repressed conflict became a conscious resolution: that she would continue to love her employer, but accept that her love would remain unrequited.

In essence, then, Freud's analysis shows that Lucy's

hysteria was exactly like my problem with the typewriter. In both cases a mental conflict which caused pain and disquiet resulted in a repression occurring which sought to resolve it. But whereas the repression which kept me in ignorance of the true cause of the typewriter breakdown ultimately weakened and failed when the occasion for it had passed, Lucy's remained, at least until Freud's pressure method helped her overcome the inner resistance which had tried to safeguard it.

Yet on a deeper level both examples reduce to much the same thing. This is because both repressions failed, and the repressed returned, directly in my case, indirectly in Lucy's. Lucy's repression failed because, although it kept conscious awareness of her conflict out of her mind, it could not prevent a disguised reminder of it – the smells – from reappearing. Furthermore, since the symptom was directly motivated by the repressed conflict, it was related to it and, in a cryptic sort of way, revealed it, as the following analogy might help to suggest.

Some years ago, when my experience of word-processors was much more limited than it is today, I noticed an apparently random string of letters and numbers appearing in the margin of the document which I was typing into a terminal. When I reported this to the technicians I realized that what I had seen was not meaningless, but a coded message revealing a fault in the terminal. In the same way, what Breuer and others might have regarded as 'insanity' or meaningless delusions produced by auto-suggestion or physical brain disease Freud understood as a coded message, revealing, as the computer code did, the nature of the fault. As a consequence, the hysterical symptom was seen as leading back via the associations and memories of the patient to the initial traumatic situation and revealing the repressed.

Thanks to this insight, Freud could conclude that 'the mechanism which produces hysteria represents on the one hand an act of moral cowardice and on the other a defensive measure which is at the disposal of the ego'. The aim of psychoanalysis, as in Lucy's case, is to substitute a bit of moral courage – a conscious resolution of a conflict – for an unconscious and irrational type of defence. It aims to put a conscious decision in the place of a compromise in consciousness; an outcome dictated by reality in place of a fantasized one nurtured by the pleasure principle.

Freud's emphasis on the dynamic nature of the conflicts underlying hysterical symptoms rather than the predisposing conditions of Breuer's approach naturally meant that it was the balance of forces involved and their characteristics which seemed important in determining the outcome of the disorder, its peculiar symptoms, and so on. In Lucy's case Freud's suspicion that there must have been more to it than just a disagreeable scene with the other members of the household arose from a not unnatural feeling that the emotions involved in that incident were hardly important enough to produce the observed result – hallucinations and other hysterical symptoms. Freud began to suspect that the repressed factor in Lucy's case – her love for her employer – was altogether typical and that erotic feelings played a major role in the causes of the psychological conflicts which could lead to the formation of symptoms.

His pressure method led him to try to get other hysterics to recall such feelings, and he was usually successful. For instance, on the occasion of his visit to the USA in 1909, his American follower Granville Stanley Hall (1846–1924) presented Freud (and Jung, who accompanied him) with a case which he was analysing where an erotic factor seemed to be totally absent. Yet following a few minutes of questioning by both Jung and Freud – the pressure method in its most inquisitorial form – the lady in question revealed the truth: a love affair was indeed at the bottom of it all!*

In Freud's view these findings were not too surprising if

*G. S. Hall, 'A Medium in the Bud', *American Journal of Psychology*, 25, pp. 149–200, 321–92.

one reflects for a moment on the great strength, urgency and importance of erotic feelings in human beings as well as on the fact – even more relevant in 1895 than it is today – that such feelings are likely to be well hidden from others and everywhere hedged about with moral, aesthetic and social constraints and conventions. One simply tends to keep one's most intimate and improper thoughts to oneself. Lucy rightly regarded her thoughts about her employer as improper and kept them to herself so effectively that even she did not know about them until they were coaxed from her by Freud. This is why we find him speaking of 'moral courage' as the alternative to the self-deceptions of hysteria. It was the reality principle's alternative to, and source of strength against, the resistance dictated by the pleasure principle.

Free association and the fall of the seduction theory

Freud's emphasis on the erotic element was ultimately to produce something for which he himself seems at first to have been quite unprepared. An unmistakable note of moral shock and personal distaste creeps into his private correspondence where he reveals the surprising finding to which his enquiries led: just about all patients reported not simply repressed erotic feelings and episodes, but repressed erotic feelings and episodes which seemed to have occurred in childhood and which suggested that they had been sexually abused by adults!

Yet, in another respect, this was just what he was looking for. Here was the fundamental sexual trauma which his theory at that time required. Because sexual seduction in childhood seemed bound to be traumatic to the child concerned and inevitably had to lead to repression (because a child cannot achieve genital sexual satisfaction of its erotic drives like an adult), it seemed to follow that such seductions had to be a universal cause of hysteria in later life when the emergence of adult sexual desires served to reactivate the early infantile trauma. This seemed to explain why so many hysterics were either young women or older ones whose marital sexual satisfaction was not all it could be. The cultural prohibition on infantile expressions of sexuality seemed to explain why such seductions were usually strenuously repressed and why so much difficulty was encountered in uncovering them.

For a year or two in the late nineties Freud pursued this idea, but with increasing dissatisfaction. Then, in September 1897 he admitted to his intimate correspondent Wilhelm Fliess (1858–1928) that he no longer believed in what, in a nice verbal play on 'neurotic' and 'erotica', he called his *neurotica*. The seduction theory fell as fast as it had risen.

There were a number of reasons. One was that he seemed unable to bring analyses to a proper conclusion and to clear them up with complete success. But much more important than this otherwise laudable candour about his own therapeutic limitations was the sheer incredulity which the theory of universal infantile seduction of neurotics brought, especially when, as Freud admitted to Fliess, his own neurotic tendencies and those of other members of his family pointed to his father as the guilty party! He evidently could not bring himself to believe that Vienna was so densely inhabited by child-abusers as his case material seemed to suggest.

Yet his scepticism had better and much deeper foundations. One of these is to be found in the technical change which he had gradually introduced in the early nineties and which, from the point of view of therapeutic method, marks the true beginning of psychoanalytic practice.

He found that even the pressure method was unnecessary if he took his basic assumption about it to its logical conclusion. Since he assumed that the unconscious exercised some influence on the processes of consciousness, albeit indirect and disguised, he reasoned that if consciousness could be freed from its normal constraints it would wander, so to speak, under no conscious control of its own, but under that of the unconscious forces which might affect it.

Perhaps an analogy will make the principle clear. Let us suppose I have a car which I suspect suffers from defective steering. I might become conscious of this in normal manipulations of the steering wheel, but as long as I am holding the car on the true course I only have subjective feelings to go on related to the forces which I am obliged to exert. If, however, I can find a stretch of wide, straight and level road I might temporarily take my hands off the wheel and let the steering reveal any innate bias of its own, so that, for instance, if the car suddenly veers off to the side I can be sure that something is wrong.

In a similar way, Freud found that if conscious direction of thought is suspended and the patient is encouraged to report trains of thought which are allowed to wander where they will without any interference by patient or analyst then the latent, compulsive tendencies of the unconscious will begin to be revealed. This technique, called *free association*, rapidly supplanted the earlier pressure method, just as the latter had replaced hypnotism as the prime method of what was now psychoanalysis proper.

Now the patient remained comfortably on the analytic couch, but the analyst retreated out of view. Seated at the head of the couch, able to see the recumbent patient, but only visible if the latter were to rise and turn, the analyst sought to produce as near as possible complete freedom from any kind of restraint on the patient's free associations, even those which might inadvertently register in the face or person of the analyst. Relaxed, unpressurized and encouraged to let their thoughts wander freely, patients could almost imagine that they were quite alone, verbalizing the unconscious to empty space.

The analyst in turn now renounced pressure and directive questioning for an attitude complementary to that of the patient: one of free-floating attention not constrained by any particular expectation or intention. Even the taking of notes during the analytic hour was avoided because of the disturbance and selectiveness of attention which it inevitably entailed. The persistent questioning and encouragement of the earliest period now gave way to a method which was primarily one of listening, with only the occasional question of clarification and aptly timed interpretation to impede the flow of associations, which often might continue uninterrupted for the entire analytic hour.

Although free association thus became the principal technical innovation of therapeutic psychoanalysis, there is no reason why it should be limited to therapy alone. As we shall see in the next chapter, anyone who wishes to uncover the latent meaning of dreams can do so by use of this method, and it is one which lends itself to a simple illustrative exercise which readers can try for themselves. Let me, by way of example, recount what happened the last time I attempted to demonstrate the technique to a group of students.

The class in question took place immediately after lunch one afternoon. Having reached a comparable stage in my exposition of the basic principles of psychoanalysis to that found here, I suggested that my students might carry out an exercise in free association as homework and demonstrated the technique by doing it myself on the spot. The method is as follows: without any kind of fore-thought or preparation one merely jots down a string of numbers, chosen at random. The string can be as long or as short as one likes, but experience teaches that between four and a dozen numbers are usually enough and that many more than this tend to become unmanageable.

Having written down the numbers, one then looks at them and, without exercising any kind of censorship or rational control of one's thinking, allows ideas concerning them to occur spontaneously. In the case of my demonstration I produced a list of six digits, quite without any conscious intent – I merely scribbled them up on the blackboard as they came to mind. Having cautioned the class that I might not be able to report all my associations in such a public forum, but would try to be as candid as possible, I then pursued my associations out loud.

The first thing that I noticed was that the digits I had written seemed to group themselves into three sets of two each. Readers who try the exercise for themselves will probably find a similar effect – one simply does not associate with all of them at once (although, in principle, one might, especially for short series such as those which recall telephone numbers). I then noticed that the first two digits reminded me of an abbreviated date of a year (i.e., one without the century-defining digits), and so did the second; but, for a moment, I could make no sense of the third couple of numbers.

I concentrated on the first two sets and immediately saw a link. The two dates in question were years of my life when major changes had occurred relating to my career; but the third set still puzzled me. At this point I was prey to a feeling that will almost certainly afflict any readers who try this exercise for themselves. Like most people, I found that when it was a question of finding further associations beyond the first a feeling of disbelief and scepticism assailed me, as if I were 'making it up' as I went along, 'inventing it' for the benefit of the class.

But, like the reader who wishes to succeed in this task, I made myself realize that such objections are typical and must be resolutely ignored. They represent the intrusion of conscious, rational criticism and have no place in free association which, by definition, is characterized by being exempted from any kind of criticism whatsoever – even that which attempts to portray such free associations as arbitrary contrivances. Despite such feelings of resistance I persevered, commenting to the class that an invention or apparently forced link is still an association, and deserves to be taken seriously.

(Readers who try this for themselves will almost certainly be assailed by resistances of various kinds. Most common are profusion of associations, which are too confused and numerous to appear to make sense; absurd, obscene or morally objectionable associations which seem intolerable; or no associations at all, which seem to make the whole task impossible. But those who find such feelings of resistance a real problem might try to circumvent them by a variation based on the pressure method in which they imagine that associations are being forced upon them by someone with a gun to their head. Even under these imaginary conditions perfectly valid free associations will probably emerge whose internal, unconscious logic can later be interpreted. In this variation the feeling of being forced merely counters the resistance; it cannot affect the unconscious compulsion for the simple reason that it is always latently present.)

Resistances aside, as far as the last couple of digits were concerned, the only association I could find was with my age at my next birthday. No sooner had I said this than the whole thing became crystal-clear. I was able to see the associations in their entirety and able to give the class a complete and uncensored account of them. Although I had subjectively felt that my final association was 'scraping the barrel' (as readers will who use the pressure variation above), it now appeared to clinch the matter. The complete interpretation was as follows.

At lunch that day I had been discussing one or two exciting possibilities relating to my future career with a colleague. When the time for my class came I had to break off the discussion in the interests of teaching my students, and consciously suppress the stimulating train of thought to which it had given rise. Yet the moment I relaxed conscious control of my thoughts in the minor matter of writing down an apparently random series of numbers the suppressed train of thought instantly reappeared. In effect it used the opportunity of an ostensibly free choice of numbers to say, 'In 19wx and 19yz important changes in your career occurred; you would like a similar kind of change by the time of your next birthday, when you will be *nm* years old. Since a string of obvious dates will encounter the censorship of your consciousness, let us disguise them by abbreviation and represent the last idea – your coming birthday – not by a date but by your age: the numbers must be *wx/yz/nm*.'

In retrospect, then, the random number-writing exercise shows that the digits produced were anything but random. Yet their latent meaning could only be reached by means of free associations which might have seemed contrived or absurd while I was pursuing them but which made perfect sense when seen in their complete context. So it is with all such number-series; and even if most of my readers are not fortunate enough to be able to carry out such a complete analysis of such a simple case as this one, they will probably find that they can pursue enough associations far enough to realize that such numbers are never randomly associated as far as the unconscious is concerned.

Looked at from another point of view, the number-writing exercise is closely comparable to my earlier example of the typewriter breakdown. In that case a suppressed wish took advantage of a lapse in attention to sabotage my weekend writing activities and then censored memories which would have enabled me to correct the fault, at least until the critical period was over, when it finally relented. In the case of the free association demonstration the temporary suspension of conscious direction of thought involved in trying to think of avowedly random numbers gave a comparably suppressed wish a chance to express itself in terms of the actual numbers chosen.

Yet it is important to notice that the underlying thinking relating to dates in my past life, my next birthday and so on had not actually occurred to me at the conscious level during my lunch-time conversation. The fact that my associations revealed them in the number-series suggests the operation of unconscious trains of thought quite unknown to me until evidence of them appeared. It seems that just as I was unconsciously able to censor and limit my memory of relevant facts in the typewriter incident, so here I was able to elaborate pertinent memories, provide definite dates and even formulate a distinct wish relating to the future – and all without any conscious knowledge or intent.

From yet another point of view, the analysis of the number-series I produced in the class is closely comparable to Freud's dynamic view of hysteria. As in the case of hysterical symptoms, the seemingly meaningless details of the series were revealed to be a manifest expression of a latent, unconscious content to which they were linked by chains of apparently arbitrary associations. Like the hysterical symptom, the numbers actually chosen provided a disguised, coded expression of something which had been excluded from consciousness, but which still evidently struggled for expression (and which resembled the word-processor code example very closely indeed). The only significant difference is that in the case of my free association demonstration the suppressed train of thought would otherwise have been consciously accessible, whereas in that of the hysterical symptom such conscious access is more or less permanently denied.

Freud's use of free association, like my classroom exercise above, immediately revealed a whole new dimension of mental life: the dynamics of fantasy. (In effect, my 'random' numbers were a fantasy about my career prospects because, whereas the first four digits referred to past events which could be represented by actual dates, the last two referred to an aspiration related to the future and were distinguished by being represented, not by dates as such, but by an age which I had not yet reached. In other words, they expressed a wish, dictated, as all such wishes are, by the pleasure principle.)

Now, free to think anything which came into their heads, Freud's patients began to fantasize, as people inevitably will if given permission to allow their thoughts to wander. In the course of these apparently incoherent wanderings many of the same things began to appear as had shown themselves under the pressure technique, in particular, scenes of sexual seduction in childhood. But their appearance in fantasy inevitably began to compromise their previous role in reported 'memory'. Under pressure from the analyst the recalling of distressing infantile sexual traumas was credible, but their spontaneous appearance in fantasy was not. Why should anyone who had had such an experience want voluntarily to recall it in fantasy? What was happening to repression? Was it so easily circumvented by free association? And what had become of traumas? How could such unpleasant experiences now become confused with wish-fulfilments?

Freud was increasingly sceptical, but gained from the experience 'the certain insight that there are no indications of reality in the unconscious'* and concluded that what he had at first taken as real events recollected under pressure were, often at least, fantasies founded not so much on the actual perverse behaviour of parents, but on the latent sexual feelings of his patients. This seemed to attribute the perversion in question to themselves as children rather than to their parents.

Although temporarily disorientated by the fall of his fondest theory, Freud had just taken the first and major step towards one of his most momentous and controversial discoveries: infantile sexuality in general and the Oedipus complex in particular. Expressed in other terms, he had found that what at first he regarded as a consequence of reality was in fact the product of the pleasure principle. It was this contamination with wish-fulfilment which finally discredited the seduction theory and suggested that the facts regarding human sexuality and mental life were not so simple or so straightforward as they might have seemed. Furthermore, with the pleasure principle to contend with it was inevitable that the struggle to establish the reality was

The Complete Letters of Sigmund Freud to Wilhelm Fliess, ed J. Masson (Cambridge, Mass., 1985), p. 264.

bound to be more difficult than the seduction theory might have led him to suppose. Yet, fortunately for him, he was simultaneously starting out on what he was later to call 'the royal road to the unconscious': the interpretation of dreams. Here once again fact and fantasy were to be inextricably intertwined and here too free association was to be the key which was to unlock the secret.

3

Dreams

Dream-interpretation and self-analysis

The later 1890s were significant in the development of psychoanalysis for more than one reason. Quite apart from his pioneering psychotherapeutic work with hysterics, Freud was developing two other important lines of enquiry into the hidden workings of the human mind. These were his *Interpretation of Dreams*, published late in 1899, and his self-analysis.

Writing to his friend Wilhelm Fliess in 1897, Freud called his 'self-analysis . . . the most essential thing I have at present' and added that it 'promises to become of the greatest value to me if it reaches its end.'* Its end was to be the same as that to which his exploration of dreams and hysteria was leading: the discovery of infantile sexuality and its principal focus in the Oedipus complex.

As the first person ever to carry out a systematic self-analysis along psychoanalytic lines, Freud's achievement was unique. Once he had discovered Oedipus in himself, anyone else who did so was merely following in his trail-blazing footsteps. But precisely because he did blaze the trail, following it is by no means impossible. So rather than repeat well-known explanations and examples of Freud's

The Complete Letters of Sigmund Freud to Wilhelm Fliess, ed. J. Masson (Cambridge, Mass., 1985), p. 270.

own, let me, by way of contrast, attempt to show how, using his method of dream-analysis, one can penetrate some considerable way to the hidden meaning of one's own dreams.

Another reason for adopting this approach is that the analyses of dreams contained in Freud's classic work are mostly incomplete and fragmentary, all except one produced to illustrate some particular aspect of dreams and the processes which produce them. This is even true of the one apparent exception, the famous 'specimen dream'. Unfortunately, not even this pursues the analysis as far as it would be possible and so fails to represent anything like a completely elucidated dream. Freud himself had wanted to include an example of a more fully completed dream-analysis, but we have Fliess to thank for the fact that he was prevailed upon to delete it from the published text.

Such dreams are difficult to find, mainly because of the indiscretions involved in revealing anything like a complete analysis, as Fliess evidently realized. Nevertheless, in his private self-analysis Freud had no such problem and no such vulnerability to good advice. There he could convince himself by following chains of associations to their end, but relied on his monumental *Interpretation of Dreams* to convince others by piecemeal demonstrations of the basic mechanism of dreams.

My approach is to repeat what he did, using specimen dreams of my own, but not to hold back so much of their complete analysis. I propose to use the classical method of free association whereby, having recounted the remembered, so-called *manifest dream*, I then supply my associations much as I did in the random number-writing exercise in the last chapter. This approach has the advantage of embarrassing no one but myself and violating no confidences of others. It carries a further weight of conviction, I believe, which general theoretical explanations or second-hand case material lacks.

Anyone who attempts to analyse their own dreams will

soon discover that dream-interpretation is basically a moral issue; fundamentally, it is a question of the extent to which one can be honest about one's own unconscious. It is really an exercise in recognizing ourselves as we would never allow others to see us. In this undertaking second-hand goods lack the hallmark of authenticity, and reading about other people's dreams cannot be a substitute for the shock of discovering the hidden meaning of one's own. So, since my readers have to accept some account, I have tried to make mine as authentic as possible and would certainly hope that, having seen how it is done, they might try it for themselves. As Freud pointed out to Fliess regarding his own self-analysis, 'Being totally honest with oneself is a good exercise.'*

As a preliminary to the main example which I want to consider, let us begin with the following dream which has the virtue of being extremely simple and purely verbal, having a manifest content in the form of a single sentence.

One night many years ago I went to bed and within minutes of falling asleep had the following dream: *I seemed to hear a voice loudly and distinctly saying, 'They tow your wife away!'*

Just as Freud found that the manifest symptoms of hysterics could be traced back to their unconscious, latent causes by following chains of free associations, so he found that associations with the manifest content of a dream could be followed back to an otherwise unknown and repressed *latent* content. As an example, let us take the dream just recounted, and, as a method, let us use the very same approach illustrated earlier in connection with the random number-writing which I demonstrated for my class.

The first thing which occurred to me when I allowed my thoughts to form spontaneously in relation to the dream was a so-called *day's residue*: the memory of an event which had occurred on the day of the dream. This was that

*Ibid., p. 272.

someone had told me that *her car had been towed away despite being legally parked outside her own home*. This, obviously, related to the idea of something being *towed away* and provides the verb for the sentence which constitutes the manifest dream.

As far as its object was concerned, I was at first perplexed. Whose wife was being 'towed away'? It hardly seemed to make any sense in connection with my own wife. But then something else occurred to me. I noticed that the use of the phrase *your wife* in the dream seemed to suggest the less colloquial but more grammatically exact rendering *one's wife* – as if the wife concerned were that of the speaker. This immediately raised the question of who the speaker was, and here I found that the voice, so distinct and prominent in the dream, seemed to be one which I knew. I immediately thought of my father, but it seemed to sound younger. Then I thought of my brother, but this seemed wrong. Finally, I realized who it must be: it was the voice of my father as I imagine – or remember – it to have been *when he was younger*.

With this realization, the whole meaning of the dream instantly became clear. If it was my father speaking as a younger man, *one's wife* would refer, not to his wife at the time I had the dream, but to my mother, who had died early in my childhood. In fact, on the night of the dream, just before having it, I had been thinking about my grandmother's recent death. This had been occasioned by finding a tune from a music-box which she owned going through my head obsessively as I tried to go to sleep. I recalled that the voice in the dream – evidently that of my father – had turned on and off as if it were a tape-recording, and so loud and distinct that it had woken me up. Here *a tune from my grandmother's music-box which made me recall her recent death* associates with *a memory of my father's voice as it was in the past* and on to my mother, who in the manifest dream has been mysteriously *towed away like the car on the day of the dream*.

This can only mean that, in the latent dream, the idea of my mother's death was equated with the wrongful removal of the car. This makes perfect sense if I recall that at the time of her death my grandmother was a very old woman. In fact she was already quite old when my mother died. My mother, by contrast, had died at the age of forty. With these facts in mind the idea of my mother having been wrongfully taken from me in view of her relative youth becomes perfectly clear in the context of thoughts about my grandmother's death at an advanced age.

It seems, then, as if the latent dream-thought must have been something like: 'You were recalling your grandmother's recent death but, by rights, your mother ought to have lived as long as your grandmother. Like the car you heard about today, your mother was wrongfully taken from you!' Expressed in everyday terms rather than the cryptic words of the manifest dream, it seems that I was equating a justifiable complaint made by someone on the day of the dream with a repressed, latent complaint hidden in my unconscious but stimulated into expression by the conscious memory, not of my mother's, but my grandmother's, death.

In this respect the dream is almost exactly like the random number-writing exercise discussed earlier. In both cases an apparently meaningless series of signs – in that case numbers, in this words – was found to be linked by associative chains with latent thoughts which completely explained it. The only real difference is that, in the random number case, the latent thoughts had been only temporarily suppressed, whereas in that of the dream they had not occurred to me prior to having it and even then would have remained unconscious had I not been able to analyse their hidden meaning. In this respect, as Freud himself pointed out, the dream is much more like the hysterical symptom in that it draws on the permanently repressed, dynamic unconscious, rather than on the temporarily suppressed content of the pre-conscious revealed in the number-association example.

A specimen dream

Having seen how association can be used to link manifest and latent content in the analysis of a simple dream, let us now graduate to a more representative example and carry out the same kind of operation, but with somewhat richer material. As in the previous example, I will first reproduce the manifest dream and then provide associations with the latent content.

The dream is as follows: *I am somewhere like Germany, or perhaps India, with a group of cadets or young soldiers. The particular location seems to be some kind of fair-ground or camp. A disreputable old man who looks like a tramp becomes violent and threatens us. I respond with boasts about our weapons, but we do not seem to have them with us.*

The man enters what seems to be some kind of trailer or tool-shed where he finds a hatchet. As he raises this to threaten us we barricade him in and my colleagues ram what appears to be a petrol tanker into the cabin and begin to pour petrol everywhere. I am not sure who throws the match, but in any event, the man is incinerated.

Afterwards, I reflect that I can always explain away my state of upset by saying that I was very near the explosion when it occurred. However, I notice one of my sons smirking at me and hope that he will not give away my guilty secret!

At face value, and considered solely from the point of view of its manifest content, a meaningless dream, but one which, when considered along with its associations, soon assumes a very significant meaning. Let us list these associations and see where they lead us:

Somewhere like Germany, or perhaps India I had lived in Germany with my father, who was an officer in the occupation forces, until my mother's death in 1951, when I was five. My mother had been cremated, and India I associate with *Indira* Gandhi, who had been cremated at her recent funeral there.

A group of cadets or young soldiers   It was my father, of course, who was in the army, but I was in the Combined Cadet Corps at school.

Some kind of fair-ground or camp   In Germany at the time of my mother's death we were living in a military compound on the edge of an army camp. The fair-ground I associate with a town where I went to live with my mother's relatives after her death and with another sea-side resort to which I went with my father and his sister immediately after our return to England in the summer of 1951.

A disreputable old man who looks like a tramp   This must be my father, for reasons which will soon become clear. It must be admitted that this is a very unflattering portrayal of him. However, he had been violent towards my mother in the course of quarrels in Germany and had on one occasion fired a gun inside the house, the bullet going into the ceiling.

Weapons . . . we do not seem to have them   This I associate with another episode I can remember in which I discovered some bayonets in our house in Germany and ran brandishing one into the room, only to be immediately disarmed by my father.

Some kind of trailer   The trailer suggests one belonging to Field Marshal Montgomery which I had seen at the Imperial War Museum; the *tool-shed* I associate with the shed at the bottom of my father's garden.

I am not sure who throws the match   This recalls an alarming event at school, when I was 18. A group of us had been detailed to tidy up the classroom and had collected a large metal waste-paper basket from outside to expedite the job. Soon it became full of paper. Then someone – definitely not I – threw an unextinguished match into it. Immediately it caught fire and flames began to rise towards the ceiling. Reluctant to use a fire-extinguisher for fear of being found out, the four or five of us present – who, fortunately, had not had a chance to leave the classroom after morning school – made use of the same method as Gulliver did in putting out the fire at the palace in Lilliput, no other source of water being available within easy reach. This quickly extinguished the fire, which, luckily for us, was never detected by the authorities.

The man is incinerated As I mentioned before, my mother was cremated, but so was my father when he died some few years ago. At that time I was the one responsible for the funeral arrangements and had led the mourners.

Afterwards I reflect that I can always explain away my state of upset by saying that I was very near the explosion This suggests a need for an excuse, and therefore a sense of guilt, a suppositon confirmed by the final associations:

I notice one of my sons smirking and hope that he will not give away my guilty secret Two or three days earlier one of my sons had told tales on his brother. The latter had smirked guiltily as his confidence had been violated. In the context of the dream my son's misdemeanour is equated with my knowledge that I have been instrumental in committing a murder and strongly suggests what all the previous associations already indicate: namely, that the secret I wish no one to suspect is that I have murdered my own father!

Here the reader, like my conscious mind, is likely to scoff and to observe that, since my father died of natural causes, I cannot possibly *really* feel any guilt. What the dream shows is what everyone thinks they know: that dreams are unreal and absurd and should not be taken seriously by any sensible human being.

Perhaps; but consider the following line of reasoning. In one way, the dream does tell the truth because it is a fact that I did have my father enclosed in a wooden box and I did burn his body. Admittedly, this was after he was dead and in circumstances where his death could not possibly be attributed to any action of mine; but the fact remains that I did do these things. That the dream seems to equate my cremation of my father with my son's guilty smirk suggests that some latent guilt associated with my father may have been present. It seems that, even though I did not in fact bring about my father's death, something in me *might have wished that I had done.*

In other words, we have come, merely by following my associations with the manifest dream elements, to the same conclusion at which Freud arrived following his use of free association in the analysis of neurotics: the discovery that mere wishes can motivate an inner conflict and give rise to symptoms whose meanings can only be divined by reference to the fantasies which underlie them.

To put the matter in another way, we might say that our preliminary analysis of this dream reveals the essential insight of Freudian psychoanalysis, which is that individuals are not the passive victims of the reality around them but are engaged in actively reshaping it within their own minds. The fact that the wishes which underlie this reshaping of reality are often completely unconscious ensures that, when given an opportunity, perhaps by way of some fortuitous event like a death, they set up inner conflicts from which the mind seeks to defend itself by all kinds of means, among which, evidently, is to be numbered the creation of dreams.

The dreamwork

In the case of dreams Freud argued that everyday events trigger unconscious wishes which then struggle for expression, just as Lucy's employer's initial behaviour towards her had encouraged her ultimately disavowed feelings towards him. Furthermore, just as neurotic symptoms like Lucy's hallucinations of smells could be understood as representing the repressed wishes which they replaced, so the manifest, remembered content of a dream could be seen as standing in place of a forgotten, latent content. The means by which this latent content was translated into the manifest dream was called the *dreamwork*.

Let us proceed with the analysis of my dream as a case in

point. According to Freud's findings, dreams contrive to hide their latent meaning by three principal mechanisms. My first few associations with the opening of the manifest dream will illustrate one of them, what Freud calls *condensation*.

The manifest dream-thoughts relating to the setting associate with much more extensive memories of a much more complex reality: the history of my childhood and a number of later events. They refer to Germany and to where we lived there; but they also allude not merely to my mother's death, but to the method of her disposal, to my father's profession, to my later membership of the CCF and to the two places to which I was taken immediately after her death – a fairly comprehensive history of the period. In other words, what has happened is that some very extensive latent memories and historical facts have been condensed into one dream-image so that the place where the dream takes place stands for at least three other places in reality and for numerous other facts.

Such condensations are not limited to dreams. We saw that in Lucy's hysteria a whole complex of ideas, emotions, wishes and memories had been condensed into one symptom, her olfactory hallucination. In fact such a process of condensation is typical of *conversion hysterias*: that is, those in which an entire mental conflict has been repressed and replaced by – or *converted* into – a physical symptom.

A second feature of the mechanism of dream construction is what Freud called *displacement*. This is represented in an unmistakable way by means of the association with the fire at the school. On that occasion I knew that I was not responsible for the blaze, and in the dream responsibility is shifted to someone else – I do not know who throws the match. Yet the final associations with my son's conspiratorial look and my own recognition of having some kind of guilty secret point directly in the opposite direction and suggest that it is I, not someone else, who is responsible for the death of the tramp in the fire. The manifest content of the dream may be trying to deny this.and to blame the others, but the latent content suggests only a displacement of the blame from its proper home in my own unconsious.

Such a displacement also has its hysterical counterpart. For instance, Freud relates the case of a Viennese lady who could not bring herself to walk down a particular street in the centre of the city because of an unaccountable fear – a case not of conversion, but *anxiety hysteria*. Analysis revealed the reason to be a shop bearing her husband's name immediately next door to an undertaker's. Anxiety aroused by death-wishes against her husband on account of her unhappy marriage had been displaced from their true, latent point of reference to an altogether different, manifest one.

In this example the displacement relates to an affect – anxiety – but, unlike condensation, which usually compounds different psychological factors, displacement can relate to more or less anything. An instance of the displacement of a recollection is characteristic of what is known in psychoanalysis as a *screen-memory*. Such memories comprise a manifest recollection which hides, or screens, another, latent one. Indeed, it is a finding of psychoanalysis that the important psychological events of childhood are not, in all probability, forgotten at all. It seems likely that they are only partially forgotten by giving way to screen-memories which represent them in a disguised manner reminiscent of dreams, as the following example suggests.

Although I now know that I was present during the shooting incident in Germany mentioned earlier, I retain no conscious memory of it. However, I do clearly and vividly recall something else related to a shooting in that house. I remember quite distinctly that, just before we left Germany after my mother's death, my elder brother went up with me to the shooting range which he had in the loft. There, as a final and rather delinquent gesture (motivated, for all I know, by my father's firing the gun in the latent incident), he shot the light out with his air-gun, after which we left the house forever. Associations which run parallel with many reported here in connection with the dream leave little doubt that this recollection of an event innocuous in itself stands as the conscious, manifest recollection of another, much more disturbing one which occurred in the same house somewhat earlier. Just like a piece of dream-symbolism or a psychopathic symptom, my memory of the innocuous shooting appears to stand as a compromise between the desire to recall a trauma associated with another shooting incident and the equally strong desire to forget it.

Finally, Freud found that dreams disguise the latent thoughts which constitute them by means of *distortion*. This emerges very clearly in the portrayal of my father in the dream. In reality he was most certainly not the violent, drunken tramp who is depicted there. On the contrary, as the commanding officer of the military base in question, he must have seemed to be the exact opposite. It was the destitute local population who resembled the down-and-out character in the manifest dream. Again, at the time my father was 40, hardly an old man like the one depicted here. Yet, for all that, the associations show quite unmistakably that he must be my father and that other, less creditable, less flattering perceptions of him may lurk behind his manifestly improbable appearance in the dream.

An example of radical distortion in a neurotic symptom was related to me by Anna Freud in connection with the first case which she ever analysed. Apparently the young lady in question came for analysis because she had been seen trying to strangle and/or suffocate her aged mother in the street by winding scarves and mufflers around the old lady's neck to such an extent that passers-by called the police. The young woman had been sure at the time that she was only concerned to keep her mother warm and comfortable. Analysis soon revealed antagonistic feelings towards the person who was depriving her of her youth and showed how elaborate *reaction-formations* manifestly about looking after her mother in fact hid latent death-wishes which had nearly been carried out in the incident which precipitated her analysis. By contrast to the two previous cases, such distortion of a latent instinctual wish into its exact manifest opposite is characteristic of *obsessional neurosis*.

It seems, then, that the fundamental mechanisms of the dreamwork are not limited to dreams. The laws which govern the translation of the repressed unconscious into its disguised equivalents express themselves in psycho-pathology just as readily as they do in dreams. The reason for this similarity is that both dreams and psychopathic symptoms represent the same fundamental process: what we may call *the return of the repressed*.

In both cases a consciously accessible manifest content is built on the model of a repressed latent content which it partially expresses. If repression means forgetting of a latent content, then its associated manifest content represents a partial, if heavily disguised, remembering – a latent return of the repressed.

Having now revealed what Freud called the dreamwork – the means by which latent content is transformed into the manifest dream – let us now ask ourselves whether my dream is as meaningless as it may at first have appeared. It seems not. On the contrary, it seems that we are confronted by a completely typical mixture of real memories and apparently unreal fantasies.

If we translate the latent dream-thoughts which seem to underlie the manifest dream, I appear – like Freud's and Breuer's hysterics – to be suffering mainly from reminisc-ences. I seem to be reminiscing about my childhood: about how my mother died in Germany and was cremated; about how my father was on occasions violent with her, once to the point of letting off a handgun in the house; about how I once brandished a bayonet, much to my father's constern-tion. Then I seem to switch to another set of memories: I recall a silly, but potentially disastrous, incident at school involving a fire, urination and delinquency and along with it I recall a more recent little misdemeanour by one of my own sons.

But mixed up, seemingly quite inexplicably, with these true reminiscences is one apparently untrue idea: the suggestion that, in having my father cremated, I was perpetrating something tantamout to murder! But this idea is not so irrational or inexplicable if we bring it together with the memories: I remember my mother's death and cremation; I remember my father's violent actions, once letting off a gun which could have murdered her; I recall my own brandishing of the bayonet; and then I begin to suspect its true motive – a violent wish directed against my father, the wish that he might die.

This explains why he is portrayed in the manifest dream as a disreputable person – a tramp – and might also explain the references to violence on his part, as if my unconscious were saying: 'Your father threatened your mother with a gun and on other occasions behaved violently towards her. Perhaps he killed her (he certainly cremated her); perhaps he deserves to die. If you kill him you will avenge the murder of your mother and all the other wrongs he did her. *It was your father, not your mother who should have died in Germany.*'

Now we can understand why one apparently inexplicable fantasy should have become intermingled in the dream with many true reminiscences. We can see that the dream tried to correct the memories, it tried to say that I had murdered my father in retaliation for his presumed murder of my mother and to plant this fantasy among a series of true facts rather as a dishonest dealer in antiquities might try to pass off the occasional forgery among many genuine pieces.

Comparing it to my introductory dream we find a notable parallel. In both cases it was a question of my unconscious voicing a protest about the death of my mother, but, on that occasion, motivated by thoughts in connection with my grandmother's, rather than with my mother's, death. Here the protest and its associated death-wishes seem much more strident, a fact easily explained by the wealth of associations and the considerable ambivalence which they revealed.

The excuse to which I refer in the manifest dream, *that I can always explain away my state of upset by saying that I was very near the explosion* is tantamount to the excuse which Freud's patients were making when they attributed their infantile sexual traumas exclusively to the agency of the adults who had allegedly abused them. By saying that I was upset and agitated because I was so close to the conflagration I was shifting all the responsibility for my state of mind onto the outside world and an accidental event – a trauma, if you like. I was like the patient who claimed to recall an incident of seduction in childhood. It was something which just chanced to happen to me and for which I could not be held responsible.

Our analysis of the latent thoughts reveals a deeper and less reassuring truth just as surely as Freud's analysis of his patient's seduction stories. It is not that he denied that such seductions could or had happened any more than our analysis of my dream causes us to deny the fact of my father's death or the real incidents of my childhood. It is just that such an analysis as this reveals that neurotics suffer not merely from reminiscences, but from their own reactions to them as well. As a small child, I could not help harbouring completely contradictory feelings about my father which, whilst they might make me love him, might also make me hate him and desire to inflict on him the fate which had been my mother's.

Freud's analysis of his hysterics convinced him that whether seduction did or did not occur was to some extent beside the point. The same can be said about the objective justice of my feelings of resentment and hatred against my father. Did my father abuse my mother and myself by his behaviour? Did the incident with the gun stand in relation to my death-wishes against him as alleged seductions stood to Freud's patients' libidinal desires? In a sense it did, and I would certainly be justified in claiming that my father must share some of the responsibility for my feelings, if they really originate in guilt over death-wishes against him.

Yet a great part of the responsibility is also my own. In

any case, the whole question of the objective guilt or otherwise of my father for making me harbour contradictory feelings about him is really quite beside the point if it is my own guilt which is at issue. The dream unmistakably shows that it is I who wanted to kill someone and that it is a consciousness of this which I have to hide under the excuse that I was traumatized by being so near the fire.

In other words, where an inner conflict is concerned, external blame is hardly a relevant consideration. My attempt in the dream to shift the blame just will not work. Psychoanalysis forces me to confront my own unconscious and examine the unsavoury things which I find there. Among these indubitably are death-wishes against my father.

Freud's central and most important finding with regard to dreams, namely that *every dream is the fulfilment of a wish*, is therefore the equivalent of his discovery that, in the origins of neurosis, fantasy and repressed wishes in general play every bit as important a role as objective realities like infantile seduction. He found that dreams were no more the products of passive responses to the experience of the day than hysterias were the automatic and simple outcomes of traumas.

If we refer back to my dream, the way in which I presented it certainly seems to reveal a latent wish, namely that my father rather than my mother should have died in my childhood. Yet our analysis of the dream showed that in at least one important respect the dreamwork partly failed. This failure relates to the displacement of guilt onto the other boys in general and onto the one who threw the match in particular. We can deduce that this displacement failed because at the end of the dream I am still anxious about the possibility of my guilt being revealed by my son and am imagining excuses for my agitated state of mind.

In this respect the dream resembles a class of dreams which, at first sight, seem blatantly to contradict the Freudian theory that every dream is the fulfilment of a wish.

This is the class of anxiety dreams or nightmares which seems to do anything but satisfy a wish and from which the dreamer usually awakens in a state of fright.

Freud's explanation of these apparent exceptions is that in such anxiety dreams the dreamwork progressively fails to fulfil its basic functions of safeguarding sleep. Much the same occurs in dreams motivated by pressure on the bladder. As long as dreamers do not succeed in finding the place they are always looking for in such dreams all is well, but if they do find it and fulfil the latent wish they will probably awaken in a wet bed! The inability to find the place where one can conveniently gratify one's needs in these dreams is the means by which the dreamwork attempts to safeguard sleep – a postponing tactic, as it were, in which the wish to waken and visit the lavatory is countered by a compromise: the dream offers one the same destination, but constantly frustrates one's ability to get there in order to prolong the state of sleep.

In a similar way to the dream which fails either because of satisfaction of the need while still asleep or because it cannot be gratified without waking, the anxiety dream also represents failure of the dreamwork in its prime task of safeguarding sleep, with the inevitable consequent wakening. Disturbing and frightening latent thoughts which the dream attempts to disguise break through the concealments offered by condensation, displacement and distortion and attract conscious attention, leading to waking in a state of fright.

In my dream something similar occurs. Had the dreamwork been wholly successful, anxiety about guilt would not have broken through towards the end and the dream would not have been followed by waking. The fact that the anxiety did break through suggests that some factor was operating to frustrate the dreamwork just as it may do in an anxiety dream where, for instance, the dreamer obtains a masochistic satisfaction from the anxiety-provoking situation. In this case a counter-wish to be frightened because one enjoys it contradicts another wish not to be aroused by anxiety and to continue to sleep.

Finally, dream-recollections of terrible, consciously re-called traumas also occur, often repeatedly and again in apparent total contradiction of the Freudian expectation that every dream should be a wish-fulfilment. However, in those instructive cases where the trauma – such as intern-ment in a concentration camp or prison – unfolds over a period of time, only fairly obvious wish-fulfilling dreams relating to escape, rescue, food, comfort and so on are reported to occur in the course of the experience. Recollec-tion dreams of the terror itself only set in after escape or delivery from it, supporting Freud's view that such dreams represent unsuccessful attempts to master the memories. They can be seen as fulfilling the wish to recall the traumatic events otherwise than they actually were, but always failing because of the inability of the dreamwork to disguise the traumatic quality of the original memories. Such dreams represent a return of the repressed just as much as any others, but the return of a repressed so horrifying that no amount of disguising its reality avails. In such cases, as in all other arousal dreams, the dreamwork fails; in this instance, catastrophically.

A corroborating dream

It is a fundamental finding of dream-interpretation, fully borne out by my own experience in the recording and interpretation of hundreds of my own dreams, that dreams dreamt on the same night are usually motivated by the same or closely allied wishes. Multiple dreams dreamt on the same night therefore give valuable corroboration and not infrequently extra insights into the latent wishes concerned.

Following waking from the example analysed above I fell asleep again and had the following, further dream: *I am driving my car at night accompanied by my family. The car is stationary on one side of a dual carriageway, without lights. I can see another car approaching in the distance and about to take a wrong turn onto the road where I am. Realizing that there will be a head-on collision, I fumble for the light switch, but cannot find it. Fortunately for us, the driver of the other car sees me in time and drives off down the other carriageway, gesticulating at me as he passes. I avoid his gaze and drive off, having put the lights on and reflecting that I must demonstrate that I am really a very competent driver!*

Associations: *One side of a dual carriageway . . . wrong turn* My father had once inadvertently found himself in this dangerous situation.

There will be a head-on collision On another occasion, when I was with him, he was nearly involved in a collision with another car which he had not seen. However, as in the dream, *fortunately for us, the driver of the other car saw us in time.* Not surprisingly, he *gesticulated as he passed us.*

I fumble for the light switch, but cannot find it In reality it would have been at my finger-tips, so the failure to locate it in the dream perhaps suggests a counter-wish *not* to find it.

Reflecting that I must demonstrate that I am really a very competent driver This was probably exactly how my father felt, but I also associate this sentiment with a dream dreamt some days before in which *I had accidently driven my car off a viaduct and fallen to my death.* The car I drove at the time of the dream had previously been my father's, and I had interpreted the latter dream as a death-wish related to my father's death: it seemed that I was identifying with him to the point of killing myself!

My failure to find the light switch suggests a similar suicidal wish based on a similar identification: I put myself in the same position of danger as my father and frustrate my own attempts to save myself. However, in this dream I escape injury, thanks to the other driver, just as my father did. But why should I identify with him in the first place, and why should I formulate wishes against my own life when in the previous dream I was concerned with death-wishes against his?

Our difficulty lies in accounting for the death-wish turned back against myself. In my associations I found that I kept coming back to the fumbling with the light switch which both expressed a death-wish against myself and seemed to suggest other things which might at first seem silly, irrelevant or indecent, but which, on analysis, turn out to be crucial.

In fact, the so-called light switch on my car is not so much a switch as a stalk or lever which sticks out of the steering column. When the lights are off it is horizontal, but when fully on sticks up in a rather provocative way. Furthermore, when I pursued my associations with 'switch' I was reminded of an item of decoration I had once seen which represents the naked body of a little man which can be fitted, thanks to a convenient opening, over a light switch in such a way that the switch represents his genital (either 'up' or 'down' as the case may be).

Furthermore, if I am driving my father's car and sitting in his place, the light switch associations suggest a further, sexual dimension to my identification with him, as if I were trying to do something in a sexual sense which my father had done, but yet feared to do myself. Now we see why I am driving his car – that is, putting myself in his place in a literal sense. We see why my family has to be present: this is putting myself in his place in a figurative sense which emphasizes my sexual role as a husband and father. If the other associations of the dream are taken into account they suggest a typical complex of ideas also revealed on one particularly amusing occasion by a slip of the tongue on the part of one of my sons.

Following a breakfast-table conversation with him at about the age of four as to why he could not marry his mother, and having trotted out all the usual rationalizations and excuses – she is too old for you, already married and so on – I got up from the table to leave the house. A few minutes later my son ran up to say good-bye, obviously meaning to say, 'Daddy let me kiss you'. What he actually said was, 'Daddy, let me *kill* you!' It does not seem far-fetched to me to assume that, after our conversation about why he could not marry his mother, another, unmentioned idea had come into his mind. This was the realization that, if I – his father – were to die, his mother would perhaps be free to marry him after all.

My dream makes exactly the same point. It puts me in my father's place and thereby implicitly expresses the wish of the first dream. It alludes to situations of mortal danger in which my father found himself in his car and fulfils the parricidal wish by representing its consequence: I now drive his car *because he is dead*. It seems that the general principle that dreams dreamt on the same night express the same sort of wish is vindicated (as it always seems to be) and demonstrates the deeper motive beneath the death-wish so clearly expressed in the first dream.

This wish is a sexual one identical to that which motivated my son's supremely Freudian slip. It is the completely typical wish on the part of a son that he should replace his father in his mother's bed, but transposed into a manifest situation where he replaces his father in situations where his father could – and, according to the fundamental version of the wish, *should* – have died. The fact that he sees this as implying his own death is the final admission of the correctness of this interpretation and an expression of the exquisite candour and moral sensitivity of the unconscious. In the court of the conscious the manifest crime proves culpability, but in dreams and the unconscious latent guilt is its own indictment.

4

The Libido Theory

Listening to the libido

Einstein not only changed the way we see reality by giving a new geometry to space and time analogous to the new topography of consciousness introduced by Freud, he also changed the way we see mass and energy, making one freely convertible into the other. In a similar way, Freud transformed our vision of the energies involved in the workings of the human mind with what is normally called the *libido theory*. In psychoanalysis it plays every bit as important a role as Einstein's famous $E = mc^2$ formula for mass/energy conversion.

Until the advent of nuclear weapons changed their attitude to relativity, the authorities in the Soviet Union proscribed it on the grounds that Einstein's formula contradicted dialectical materialism. In the West Freud's libido theory has suffered something of an analogous fate at the hands of popular opinion because it has been similarly misinterpreted as in some way or other subversive of morality or, at the very least, of right thinking about sex.

It seems that what most affronts us is the extension of the idea of sexuality which the libido theory represents. Freud's fundamental finding was that sex has to do with much more than just reproduction of the species, and there is little doubt that at first this discovery came as something of an unwelcome shock to him. The affront which Freud initially

65

felt, and which still evidently affects many today, was the realization that sex is a much more extensive matter than we might otherwise suppose: it is not confined to adult life and to the interests of reproduction, but exists in infancy as well. The wider interpretation of sexuality in the libido theory derives almost entirely from this fact.

That adults tend to be somewhat reticent about sex is not surprising if one reflects on the circumstances which surround sexual behaviour in a civilized society. Not only is sexuality one of our most urgent and pleasurable drives, it is also the one which can land us in more trouble from the point of view of inter-personal relations than almost any other. Shame, jealousy, fantasy and hypocrisy surround practically every aspect of the subject and there are few other issues about which people are likely to feel the need to dissimulate to a greater extent. In short, our insight into our own and other people's sexual lives is likely to be prejudiced at best, especially since where powerful inner conflicts are concerned consciousness is likely to plead the Fifth Amendment and refuse to incriminate itself by not even admitting to its own thoughts on the subject.

Yet Freud's use of the method of free association gave him a unique and previously quite unparalleled insight into the sexual lives of human beings. A simple calculation reveals a fact about Freud seldom appreciated: this is that in the entirety of human history up to that time, and probably with very few exceptions since, no single human being has ever spent so much time listening to the free and unconstrained expressions of others. No father-confessor of any age or any church could possibly have logged more hours in one lifetime and could not have operated under such favourable and free conditions.

The facts are these: we know from his own account that from the opening of his private practice in 1886 Freud saw up to eight or sometimes more patients a day, six days a week, 35-odd weeks a year more or less until the end of his life in 1939. If we make allowances for slack periods prior to his years of fame from 1905 onwards and for the duration of World War I and his last couple of years in exile, the grand total may be approximately 60,000 analytic 'hours'. After discounting such 'hours' proportionately for the fact that each is actually fifty minutes, we are still left with the figure of approximately 50,000 true hours. This conservative estimate is equivalent to 2,083 days, 297 weeks or the best part of six years of continuous listening to what people wanted to tell him! (This is almost certainly something of an under-estimate, given the fact that Freud's practice actually spanned 53 years rather than the 40 assumed above. The true figure could easily be 10–20 per cent more).

Small wonder that what he found amazed him. Of course, he found that people wanted to talk about their sexual lives, their fantasies, fears and frustrations. Since the person on the couch was told, and soon realized by actual experience, that Freud's technique demanded that the analyst too should not be censorious or judgemental but would allow the free associations to wander where they would, a unique resource was opened up. In an innovation unparalleled in previous history, a relationship existed where, in a routine and reliable way, one person could talk completely freely to another, not even constrained by the other's facial or visible physical responses. Out of sight of the person on the couch, the sparing interventions of the analyst only served to ease the flow of associations and to facilitate the fundamental freedom of thought which psychoanalysis allowed. For the first time outside of close personal relationships and informal, private encounters, one human being could communicate with another without fear of disapproval, disclosure or distraction. Not surprisingly, the subject of sex was the one where the big surprises came.

As we have already seen, the fall of the seduction theory was the first of these surprises, but many more were to follow. Once his patients were free to associate ideas without any significant restraint on how they did so, it became apparent that their sexual feelings embraced much more than the apparent concerns of sexuality with the genitals and with reproduction. Immediately it became clear that the extensive non-genital, non-reproductive connections which sex was known to have in the case of the so-called *perversions* were based on very common associations which, whilst they might be expressed as acts by perverts, were nevertheless perceived as fantasies by those given the privilege of free associating on the analytic couch.

One consequence of this was that the barrier which had previously separated 'normal' from 'perverted' sex was dissolved in something like the same way that Freud's earlier insights derived from free association had dissolved the hitherto almost hermetic separation between mental 'normality' and 'pathology'. Now it became clear that there is a sense in which we are all perverts in the unconscious because such perverse tendencies were likely to be relics of infantile sexuality which have undergone repression. Even so-called 'normal' sexual behaviour had apparent 'perverse' elements in it once one began to see what was before one's eyes rather than remain blinded by habit and convention. What was kissing but the enjoyment of an oral element in sexuality? and what did this have to do with reproduction? Popular wisdom might explain it away as a conventional prelude to even greater physical intimacy, but what was one to make of those who derived their principal sexual pleasure from kissing, licking or sucking?

Auto-eroticism and the oral stage

Let us take this example as a starting point. Freud found that the free associations of his patients kept leading back to childhood. Earlier, before 1897, he would have attributed this to an oral sexual trauma in infancy; now he took a more subtle view. This was that there was indeed a practically universal 'trauma' – weaning – but that this experience was only significant because of the previous attitude of the child itself. Being weaned would not be a traumatic experience unless one were first addicted to the breast, or, at the very least, had developed some habitual need for it. We do not miss the things we do not want. If his adult patients showed a lingering attachment to oral pleasure crudely expressed in their enjoyment of kissing and sucking as a prelude to more obvious sexual acts, then was it not likely that the reason was that the initial enjoyment of sucking at the breast had a large element of sensuality as well? Anyone who has ever seen a child sucking on a comforter or its finger purely for the pleasure and reassurance it gives can have little doubt that this is true.

In short, Freud concluded that, even though oral pleasure and nutritive need might initially be one and the same, it very quickly emerges that oral sensations can become sensually pleasurable in themselves and that such intrinsic pleasures have much to do with adult sexuality. Immediately the whole range of oral sexual perversions, not to mention many eating and drinking disorders, became transparent. It appeared that they preserved, fossilized in adult behaviour, so to speak, the earliest attachment of the sexual drive – or what, in view of this rather wider meaning which Freud gave to sexuality, we should perhaps call the *libido*.

Looked at from another point of view, the oral region could be seen as an *erotogenic zone* – a part of the body with which the libido is intrinsically associated and from which sensually pleasurable sensations arise. Further examples of such zones will be reviewed later in this chapter and in the next, but, for the present, we should notice one important fact about them. This is that the existence of erotogenic zones suggests the possibility of *auto-eroticism*: in other words, sexual pleasure derived from the stimulation of the subject's own body, by the subject. Finger- and thumb-sucking are obvious examples of auto-erotic satisfactions derived from the oral erotogenic zone, but such instances point naturally towards a further, and more refined Freudian concept, that of *narcissism*.

If we are prepared to follow Freud in considering the possibility that the sexual drive in human beings is not purely a matter of adult sexual activities which lead more or less directly to reproduction, but involves a somewhat more diffuse and complex situation like that suggested by the concepts of erotogenic zones, auto-eroticism and infantile sexuality, then we have to consider the possibility that the libido could, in principle, be present practically from birth. If it is, then an intriguing possibility is suggested: this is that in the beginning the entire person of the new-born baby could be suffused with such a libidinal charge, almost as if the whole body had become one continuous erotogenic zone.

The justification for this supposition derives from the facts of human life. Because the unborn child is in reality a part of the mother's body before birth and since its ability to distinguish between itself and the world around it is presumably initially limited and probably takes time to develop, it is not far-fetched to suppose that the libido is originally as undifferentiated as the new-born baby's ego.

Further cause for thinking this is provided by adult experiences of 'oceanic feelings' of mystical unity with nature reported by a number of distinguished authors. Such sensations might be later recapitulations of feelings which we all experienced, perhaps even before birth. If we reflect that the human foetus is in fact suspended in water, is a unity with its mother and is insulated from outside stimuli which might call on it to act as an independent organism, then we can see that such 'oceanic' feelings could reflect a real memory of an actual sensation, but one experienced too early for most of us to be able to remember.

If this line of reasoning is correct, then we can envisage the possibility that, in the beginning, there is no distinction between what we may term *object-libido*, the sexual drive directed to other objects or persons, and *ego-libido*, the libido attached to the self. The experience of birth is probably the first occasion on which the human organism is given reason to confront the possibility of a distinction between the two, and it is one which is strongly suggested subsequently by the circumstance that the objects on which it relies immediately after birth, the breast and the mother, are not always available and within reach.

Since frustration in these attachments to the outside object evidently easily leads to substitute satisfactions, such as sucking a finger in place of the nipple, it seems that we are justified in concluding that such behaviours are examples of a return to a previous condition of the libido – what we might call *primary narcissism*. This term describes the original, undifferentiated state in which the libido suffuses not only the entire body, but the mind as well.

Again, the fact that even a fundamental substitute satisfaction such as finger-sucking relies on a preliminary fantasy-equivalence between finger and nipple shows that mental operations under the influence of the pleasure principle can link external objects to their internal representations. In this way the concept of the libido becomes extended to purely internal factors, quite apart from its external attachments to objects or erotogenic zones. It is but a short step from this observation to the realization that the libido could become associated with the internal representation of the individual – the ego itself. Indeed, it was Freud's view that, just as the concept of auto-eroticism indicated that the individual's own body was the first point of attachment of the libido, so the early, undifferentiated ego was the primeval reservoir of the libido and the first libidinal stage that which corresponded to primary narcissism.

Anal and sado-masochistic

In the light of our discussion of narcissism and its relations to object-love we can see that weaning has very much greater significance as a trauma than may seem likely at first. This is because the loss of the breast with the satisfactions it brings represents the first real object-loss which the individual is likely to experience. Furthermore, if the breast and nipple were only indistinctly differentiated from the infant's own oral zone in early infancy and if attachment to the breast consequently retained a powerful auto-erotic undercurrent, we can see that this first disappointment and loss in the infant's libidinal life might represent much more than merely a frustration of the wish to suck and to satisfy a nutritive need. In many ways it represents a much more profound trauma, the shock of realizing that external object and self are not always reliably continuous and that the self, besides being the reservoir of the libido, can also be – indeed, in such circumstances may *have* to be – the object to which the libido returns when frustrated by the loss of the original object of its attachment. This concept of *secondary narcissism* corresponds to Freud's vision of the infantile ego as being like an amoeba, extending libidinal limbs to make contact with objects, but withdrawing them if the attachment cannot hold.

If we continue upwards along the path of infantile psycho-sexual development, another common childhood sexual trauma is apparent, namely toilet-training. Here again, insights derived from the libido theory make it clear that the trauma makes sense only against the background of the child's intrinsic pleasure in its excretory activities. If both retaining and voiding matter from the body can be pleasurable – and experience teaches that it can be both of these things – sensual pleasure can accrue to these activities and their derivatives just as it can to the oral erotogenic zone.

A bizarre example of libidinal pleasure in excretion is provided by the remarkable memoirs of Daniel Paul Schreber (1842–1911), a German high-court judge. Schreber suffered from paranoia to the extent of hospitalization but subsequently recovered sufficiently to secure his own release. According to his account of excretion, 'the process is always accompanied by the generation of an exceedingly

strong feeling of spiritual voluptuousness. For the relief
from the pressure caused by the presence of the faeces in the
intestines produces a sense of intense well-being in the
nerves of voluptuousness; and the same is equally true of
making water.'* With due allowances for this gifted
paranoiac's unusual prose style, we can still see that the
libidinal element shines through unmistakably, despite
being qualified by terms like 'spiritual'.

If we are prepared to allow the libido theory to include anal
as well as oral sensations, then a possible further consequence is that punishment – particularly if it is administered
to the buttocks by whips or canes – can become pleasurable
from the libidinal point of view even if physically painful.
Just as some adults derive pleasure from sucking – that is,
putting themselves in the position of a child being
suckled – so some can do the same by identifying with a
child being chastised. This seems more 'perverted' and
difficult to understand only because the pleasure in question
is partly displaced from its original anal sensations onto a
closely associated sensation – chastisement. Here the
trauma – being forced to submit to the discipline of toilet-
training – betrays the origin of the attachment which cannot
be completely given up: libidinal pleasure related to
excretion.

Just as our observations about narcissism and its relationship with fantasy alerted us to the possibility that not
merely the physical, but also the psychological, self could
become an object of narcissistic attachment, so Schreber's
mention earlier of 'spiritual' matters points out the possibility of what Freud termed *moral masochism*. Unlike the
erotogenic masochism mentioned above (erotogenic because
associated with the anal erotogenic zone), moral masochism
is entirely psychological and finds satisfaction not in

*All the quotations from the Schreber case in this chapter and the next are
from Freud's 'Psychoanalytic Notes on an Autobiographical Account of
a Case of Paranoia', *Standard Edition of the Complete Psychological Works
of Sigmund Freud* (London, 1953–1974), vol. XII, pp. 1–77.

physical, but in purely abstract suffering. As Freud pointed out, the moral masochist always turns the other cheek, hoping to receive a blow from Fate, God, Public Opinion or whatever other agency plays the chastising role.

For the moral masochist, pleasure has become completely *aim-inhibited*. What this means is that it has become divorced from its original, erotogenic source and redirected to purely psychological chastisements. Yet beneath the manifest readiness to accept psychological pain lies the original, latent masochistic pleasure, often reinforced by vigorous attachments to duty which are themselves only the adult, rationalized equivalents of the prime physical duty of early infancy: the regulation of excretion.

Strictly speaking, such masochistic satisfactions are narcissistic in quality because they relate to what is in reality self-inflicted punishment – which probably explains why moral masochists also not infrequently show signs of notable self-righteousness and moral arrogance. Cruelty towards others is perfectly compatible with cruelty towards oneself; and if the latter is narcissistically gratifying then the former can be too. The blood-stained history of Christianity shows quite unmistakably that those ready to scourge themselves are often equally ready to be the scourge of others.

If toilet-training represents a trauma in which the ego is forced by parental pressure to repudiate pleasure in its own products and internal somatic sensations, then the ego is likely to demand substitute gratifications for giving up those very pleasures. Examples abound. Forbidden narcissistic pleasure related to excretion can be partly restored by the typical *reaction-formations* to which toilet-training gives rise.

For instance, pleasure in dirt can turn into joy in cleanliness, which, since it is a defence and safeguard against the older, original pleasure as well as a self-congratulating substitute for it, must often be absurdly exaggerated to remain effective, especially since such substitute gratifications seldom achieve the degree of pleasure of the originals on which they are based. Again, coercion into conformity with adult demands about the timing of excretion can be transformed into obsessive punctuality to the point where the time-piece rules the day and its dictates become indispensable.

As far as the content, as opposed to the occasion and the quality of the anal drive is concerned, the following example provides an instance of what is probably by far the most common case: the unconscious equivalence of excrement and money.

Some years ago, when one of my sons was just beginning to toddle and to be toilet-trained, he fell over in the bedroom while getting dressed in the morning. Earlier, as was her habit at the time, my wife had sat him on the potty following breakfast, with no result. Following his little upset I sought to distract him by offering him a coin to look at. I can state quite categorically that this was the first occasion on which he had ever been allowed to handle money, since, having barely emerged from the oral stage, up to that time anything put in his hand would have immediately gone into his mouth. So, seeking to distract him by showing him the Queen's head on the coin, I let him hold it. He made no attempt to put it in his mouth. On the contrary, he looked over his shoulder at the potty, which was outside his immediate field of vision, was in the corner of the room and had not been touched for at least 15 minutes. He resolutely toddled up to it, dropped the coin into it and then, with an exultant grin which seemed to say 'Look what a good boy am I!' turned round, evidently expecting praise and appreciation rather than the laughter which greeted him from his parents.

Why had he put the coin in the potty, rather than in his mouth or anywhere else (such as his pocket)? The answer seems obvious. He had been out with his mother shopping and had often seen people thank her for giving them money and seen her thanking them for goods purchased and for change. Under the enlightened regime of toilet-training followed in our home he was rewarded with praise and approval for doing something in the potty, but never blamed for failing to do so. In his mind money and excrement were already identified as things which could win approval and which had value as a medium of exchange.

If another fundamental function of money as a unit of account is represented by the compulsive time-keeping mentioned earlier and by obsessive orderliness of various other kinds, then its function as a store of value underlies its unconscious equation with the retentive possibilities of its excremental origin. In Freud's view this could easily give rise to obstinacy and parsimony as a character-trait based on sublimated retentiveness of a valued possession of infancy, the child's stools.

In English slang, phrases like 'filthy lucre' and 'stinking rich' reflect the same anal/monetary conversion of libidinal energy, and throughout the world popular figures of speech and the more scatological details of folk-lore (such as the Neapolitan custom which required bankrupts to declare themselves by publicly defecating in a certain piazza in the city) support the psychoanalytic finding that in the unconscious excrement equals money.

The psychotic singularity

An important parallel between psychoanalysis and relativity is the fact that they share a characteristic tendency to renounce a privileged frame of reference in favour of purely relative ones. The fundamental insight of relativity was that one observer's time and distance was not necessarily exactly the same as another's, so that absolute simultaneity, for instance, could not exist. 'Now' for one observer is not necessarily 'now' for another – it could be earlier or later.

In a corresponding way, psychoanalysis relinquished any privileged, absolute frame of reference when it adopted free association as its characteristic method of research and therapy. The analyst did not insist on holding the patient to his or her or anyone else's frame of reference in the sense that anything and everything the analysand said, felt or believed was accepted at face-value and as of equal validity to anything else, the analyst's own values, thoughts and beliefs included. Just as relativity introduced a kind of temporal–spatial 'democracy' into physics in place of Newton's Absolute Space and Time, so psychoanalysis introduced a similar kind of psychic democratization in which the contradictions and convolutions of the unconscious had equal right to be considered alongside the commonplaces and certainties of the conscious.

One of the best examples of this aspect of psychoanalysis is provided by Freud's psychoanalytic notes on the case of Schreber. Freud expresses amazement that Schreber's psychiatrist, quoted in his autobiography, should have voiced criticism of Schreber's lack of tact, aesthetics and refinement in reporting his illness. Freud makes the reasonable remark that such criticisms are out of place in a case history which aims to give an honest and objective account of a severe mental illness. Freud, by contrast, adopts the relativity of viewpoint characteristic of psychoanalysis and abstains from judgement, intent instead on trying to understand him. In the course of his analysis he attempts to reveal the logic of Schreber's extraordinary delusions and to find the latent reality hidden below the manifest absurdity.

Schreber's illness began, as so many comparable cases do, with a severe hypochondria. According to the findings of psychoanalysis, such obsessive concern with one's own health reflects a narcissistic trend in the libidinal organization; one which withdraws libido from objects and directs it back again to the self, represented in this case by the body. The notable self-concern of invalids is a reflection of the same situation, but one motivated by real, as opposed to imagined, illness.

Following the hypochondria, Schreber developed delusions of persecution at the hands of his psychiatrist, Dr Flechsig, whom he described as a 'soul-murderer'. He became suicidal and began to hear voices. The sun, trees and birds spoke to him; he began to commune with God. He discovered that the latter was rather obtuse where living humans were concerned, being habituated to intercourse with the dead. God spoke the so-called 'ground-language', a rather antiquated and euphemistic German. He was the origin of plots against Schreber which involved the latter's impregnation by divine 'rays' (the 'nerves of God') which would turn him into a woman so that he could give birth to a new race of men who would redeem the world.

Even such a short account as this makes the reader begin to be aware of one of the principal features of the case, Schreber's *megalomania*. This was reflected in the fact that God, normally uninterested in the living and at an immense distance from the universe he had created, could not resist the attractions of Schreber's 'nerves' and was constrained against the divine will to make 'nerve-contact' with him. Schreber claimed to be the most remarkable human being who had ever lived and equated his role as Redeemer with that of Christ. Even his visits to the lavatory occasioned 'divine miracles' and revealed a vindictive conspiracy inspired by God which resulted in someone else always being there whenever he wished to go!

According to Freud's view, megalomania reflects a libidinal over-valuation of the ego, which adopts itself as a love-object of supreme value. Yet because it is the ego itself which is the object of its love, such an attachment is narcissistic in quality. Libidinal over-valuation can, of course, be directed towards an outside object; but in Schreber's case there was no object save Schreber himself.

One manifestation of this relates to our earlier discussion of erotogenic zones: Schreber's assertion that, whereas men only have 'nerves of voluptuousness' in and around the genitals, his transformation by God into a woman had covered his entire body in such erotogenic zones – a delusion which suggests a powerful resurgence of infantile auto-eroticism.

If Schreber's megalomania represents the positive side of the libidinal aggrandizement of his ego, another characteristic symptom represented its negative side. This was his belief that the world was coming to an end and that he was 'the only real man left alive'.

Looking at this delusion from Schreber's perspective, Freud realized that, as is always the case, such statements have a real meaning. They only appear meaningless when judged from the frame of reference of the objective, external world. But when considered in the reference-frame of the psychotic's unconscious, where fantasy, and not reality, reigns, such an end-of-the-world idea reflects a real situation: the inevitable withdrawal of libido from outside reality which the narcissistic aggrandizement of the ego entails. This effect corroborates the quantitative view of psychoanalysis that libido, like all other quantities in the real world, is limited and cannot be indefinitely extended. More here means less there; and so the impoverishment of reality to the point of the ending of the world as he knew it was the inevitable consequence of Schreber's narcissistic withdrawal into himself.

We can begin to see that the relativity of viewpoint characteristic of psychoanalysis breaks down the hitherto largely water-tight barriers set up between pathology and so-called normality. Furthermore, an understanding of Schreber's end-of-the-world delusion from the point of view of his unconscious shows that such a situation of almost total narcissistic withdrawal into the self has a clear parallel in everyday experience. Whenever we settle down to sleep our achievement of that blissful state of unconsciousness is conditional on our first withdrawing our attention from reality. The observation that outside disturbance or internal excitation can prevent us sleeping demonstrates that such withdrawal is both essential and, in the temporary conditions related to sleep, completely normal.

However, progressive unconscious withdrawal from reality during waking life of the kind seen in the Schreber case is highly pathological and results in the ego losing touch with reality in a way which, in Freud's view, is characteristic of insanity. Paranoias like Schreber's and the schizophrenias into which they often deteriorate represent a catastrophic inward collapse of the libido which suggests a final, striking analogy with relativity.

Einstein's 'democratization' of frames of reference created the possibility that conditions might exist where a body became so massive that its weight could overcome the repulsive forces of the material of which it was made, resulting in its catastrophic collapse into a dimensionless point occupying no space at all, a so-called *singularity*. Inside the *event-horizon* which surrounds such a collapsed body the escape velocity – the speed necessary to overcome its gravitational attraction – exceeds that of light itself, resulting in the space–time around it becoming so highly curved that it effectively becomes a self-enclosed region from which nothing – not even light – can escape. Within it, as seen from outside, clocks grind to a halt and time itself stands still. Outside it, as seen from inside, clocks accelerate to the point where the entire future elapses and time and the universe rush headlong to their end.

Such a gravitational 'black-hole' suggests a striking parallel with Freud's vision of the dynamics of psychosis. According to the libido theory, narcissistic withdrawal could ultimately lead to the ego retreating within the psychological event-horizon which normally insulates the unconscious from reality to the point where it produced a mental equivalent of catastrophic gravitational contraction – a psychotic singularity in which the ego collapsed into itself and lost all contact with the outside world which, seen from within, had already come to an end.

5

The Oedipus Complex

Parent–offspring conflict

Following the first two stages of psycho-sexual development, Freud found that there was a third, crucial one
between the ages of four and six or seven, which he called
the *phallic* or, alternatively, the *Oedipal period*. He used the
latter term because it alluded to the myth of Oedipus, who
murdered his father and married his mother, and the former
because his researches led him to believe that parricidal and
incestuous motives could be discerned in connection with
the culminating stage of infantile sexual development when
the libido finally became associated with the genitals. Of all
the stages of development, this turned out to be the most
important because it most directly related to adult sexuality
and character and was a crucial prefigurement of the final,
genital phase of adolescence.

   He found that what oral and anal/urinary sensations were
to the first two stages, genital sensations were to this one.
These sensations arose spontaneously during childhood and
during manual stimulation of the genital region, so that
masturbation became the pre-eminent example of auto-
eroticism. He also found that these sensations were typically
related to libidinal feelings directed, in the first place at least
and in the case of both boys and girls, towards the person of
the mother. Such masturbation was phallic in the case of
both sexes in the sense that it did not result in genital

orgasm and, in the case of girls, was related to the stimulation of the clitoris, an anatomical equivalent of the penis.

A little later in the typical course of development, the little girl switched the target of her amorous feelings from her mother to her father, thereby constituting the rather involved character of the female Oedipus complex. Freud rejected the suggested term 'Electra complex' in order to draw attention to this unique characteristic of the development of the girl which results in her phallic period being anything but the simple equivalent of that of the boy. This has led to the widespead acceptance among followers of Freud that female sexuality is a more complex and less easily understood phenomenon than its male equivalent (despite, or because of, the fact that many leading analysts have been women themselves).

Of all the findings of psychoanalysis, there is no doubt that it was Freud's discoveries relating to the Oedipus complex which were most controversial. Of course, if the theory is correct, this is just as it should be. The dominant, 'official' view of sexuality is that of adults, who feel that they have a natural right to it and think that they understand it. But many is the child who has noticed that, in its conflicts with its parents, the latter seem not to show much evidence of remembering how *they* felt as children.

Yet free association with its kaleidoscopic frames of reference shows a different view. Here, it seems that the unconscious never forgets and that its retrospective impressions, presented as fantasies, memories or dreams as the case may be, reflect a child's view of sexuality and of its relations with its parents.

At the time Freud first put forward his findings regarding infantile sexuality – in 1905, the same year that Einstein published his first paper on relativity – the very fact of sexuality in infancy was denied and the suggestion that it existed taken as outrageous and evidence of some pornographic intention in Freud and his early followers. Today this is much less true. Infantile sexuality is such an obvious fact to anyone who has ever observed young children that it is seldom denied. Who today would claim that if adults manipulate their genitals for pleasure this is unmistakably masturbation, yet if a child does exactly the same thing it is not? And who, furthermore, would claim that children do not routinely behave in this way? The answer is: no one who knows anything about children or who can recall being a child.

Yet although prudery about infantile sexuality is now much less common – if by no means unknown – the major twentieth-century view continues to be the parent's and the adult's rather than the child's. Influential social theories teach that the Oedipus complex, if it exists at all, is a product of the family setting or social environment and alleges that it is not found in some primitive societies. Other – essentially anti-Semitic – theories hold that since Freud was Jewish and so predominantly were his patients (although in all probability they were not), only Jews could be disgusting enough to lust after their mothers. This is about as sensible as saying that relativity is a 'Jewish' or 'bourgeois' science, and therefore must be wrong (an attitude which in no small part contributed, fortunately, to the Nazis and the Soviets failing to acquire nuclear weapons during World War II).

Modern views of this matter have been prejudiced by so-called *cultural determinism*, a school of thought which assumes that adult culture is the determining factor in child-development and that 'nurture' rather than 'nature' is what legislates for human behaviour. When Freud first developed psychoanalysis the situation was exactly the other way round – in other words, it was 'nature' rather than 'nurture' which was mainly credited with the dominant role in constituting character and behaviour.

Because he went out of his way to contradict this one-sided approach, he has been widely misunderstood as emphasizing nurturing factors in much the same way as cultural determinism did. Yet Freud did not find that culture determined human nature. On the contrary, the chief finding of psychoanalysis was that human nature is remarkably incorrigible and that children have their own motives – sexual ones included – which often came into direct conflict with the culture of the parents. Freud's view was one of a dynamic conflict between nature and nurture, not one of one-sided instinctual or cultural determinism.

Cultural-determinist theories of child-development, which see the infant as a passive victim of child-rearing practices and to which Freud's early seduction theory still appeals, do violence to the reality both of children and of family life. We all have families and we have all been children. We know from personal experience that family life is not harmonious and that children are not puppets whose strings can be pulled at will by the parents or their abstract embodiment in such things as the 'social environment' or 'culture'. We know from bitter experience that this is seldom, if ever, true. We know that the family is the quintessential breeding-ground for resentments, hostilities, jealousies and conflicts of all kinds. We know – especially if we have been parents ourselves – that children are not passive victims, but often the active aggressors in family affairs and that child-rearing, far from being a harmonious process of 'socialization', is in fact a battle between the very often opposing demands of the parents and the wishes of the child. Food, pocket-money, bed-times, waking-times, television, outings, homework, clothing and appearance, cleanliness and tidiness – all these and many more are issues over which parental and infantile interests usually clash, often with verbal and emotional (not to mention the occasional physical) conflicts.

A prime example of such conflict is provided in the memoirs of the painter Salvador Dali. He claims not to have submitted to toilet-training until the age of eight and reports that, until then, he habitually defecated anywhere he thought fit – on the stairs, in bed, inside cupboards, under the dining-room table, and so on. However, by way of a fiendish refinement he occasionally and secretly used the W.C. Unable to find that day's offering, for days afterwards no one else in the household could open a drawer, look under a chair or into a wardrobe without apprehension at what they might find! Here indeed is an extreme example of anal-sadism which illustrates the point that the aggressors are not necessarily always the parents and that the child need by no means always be the passive victim of their domination.

Considered from this point of view, one cannot help noticing that the conventional, sociological, non-dynamic attitude seems to favour the perspective of the parents and that the dynamic, psychoanalytic one appears to restore the balance in favour of the child.

Parental investment and Oedipal behaviour

It is in the more realistic setting of parent–offspring conflict that the Oedipus complex unfolds. Since the mother is the main provider of parental care in early childhood, it is perhaps natural that she should be found to be the early and archetypical figure of emotional attachment for the child. After all, the child was once a part of her and even after birth remained intimately dependent on her for some time in the matter of sustenance. Because human childhood is comparatively so long and human infantile development correspondingly slow, dependency on the parent – especially the mother – is both intense and crucial to the child's survival.

At first this dependency is, admittedly, almost completely passive; but soon even very young babies master the art of smiling and can begin to relate actively to the parent. Such active reactions do much to strengthen and expand the infant–parent tie and, as the child grows older, positive responses which began as facial expressions deepen into emotional feelings. A child who shows love and affection is more likely to receive these very things from its parent, and so it is by no means strange that children should try to exploit such ploys in their relations with their mothers and fathers.

In adult life we commonly accept that a smile exchanged between persons of the opposite sex can lead to a more obviously sexual conclusion. Furthermore, it seems that, since adults are susceptible to seduction, especially if it is mild and implies no immediate sexual commitment, children might be able to exploit such approaches too – after all, children have a great advantage: everyone knows that they are innocent! In short, it seems that the length and complexity of human childhood means that children might exploit emotional and sexual cues in trying to solicit parental care and, assuming that the parents were sexually normal (which on average they would be), it might pay a child preferentially to target the parent of the opposite sex. This is especially true in later childhood, when the person of the father usually becomes much more important, so that the peculiarity of the female Oedipus complex in switching from mother to father as prime target might be explained.

Nevertheless, another central finding of psychoanalysis, constitutional human *bisexuality*, may also in part be a product of this situation. Here bisexuality means the presence of both feminine and masculine elements in persons of both sexes – something indicated surprisingly early on in Freud's researches into the unconscious.

Although one sexual orientation usually predominates, evidence of the presence of the other is often betrayed in fantasies, dreams and free associations, so that Freud became convinced that it was completely normal for human beings of either sex to contain unconscious traces of the other. If such latent bisexuality was detectable in the unconscious, it followed that it was also likely to have been laid down along with most other apparently perverse and 'unnatural' sexual tendencies in the course of childhood. The following line of reasoning may begin to suggest how.

Since the child needs the love and investment of both parents for its physical and psychological well-being, the child needs to reflect positive emotional attitudes back to both. If passionate devotion to the mother on the part of the son can elicit preferential treatment in return, then there is no reason why devotion to the father should not also be a practicable tactic. A slightly different kind of approach may be better suited to fathers, who might interpret seductive behaviour towards the mother as unacceptable if directed towards themselves. A more masculine, active approach to the mother, but a more feminine, passive one to the father, might establish a life-long precedent in the unconscious. Similarly, a little girl in the Oedipal period might find that somewhat different behaviour paid off best with each of the parents.

These differential responses on the part of the child would probably not be conscious; and even if they were the need to disguise their self-interested foundation might tend to make the child disavow and repress them. Once submerged in the dynamic unconscious, infantile ambiguities about sexual role might remain unalterable throughout later life, tending to colour the sexual behaviour of the adult and to provide an unconscious, infantile foundation to later developments.

In short, being one kind of male or female to the mother and another kind to the father during childhood could establish fundamental precedents for later life and sow the seeds of future conflicts in children of either sex. If Oedipal behaviour results in a crisis of sexual identity for the child, the pre-Oedipal attitudes can be counted on to re-appear whenever such a crucial identity is tested to destruction or undergoes regressive disintegration for any reason.

Such an approach as this to the problem in terms of parental investment was not possible during Freud's lifetime, but it might explain another strange finding of Freudian psychology, the phenomenon of *penis-envy*. This term describes a latent envy of the male's possession of the penis on the part of the female and was nicely illustrated by a case which Anna Freud once related to me. It concerned a little girl whose psychological problem centred on her conflicts relating to her sexual identity. One day she arrived for her session and triumphantly announced that she did not want to be a boy any longer – that really was absurd! When Anna Freud enquired what she would like to be instead she replied, 'A giraffe!' Subsequent analysis confirmed the obvious conclusion: her wish had shifted from wanting to be a male to wanting to possess the phallic attribute which went along with being one (and which evidently was suggested by the unusually long neck of the giraffe).

Cases like this seem strange at first but become much more comprehensible when set against our modern understanding of their probable biological background. This is the realization that, as far as the preferred sex of offspring is concerned, males are preferentially valued over females in most human societies. Almost certainly this is for the simple biological reason that a successful male can leave many more descendants and therefore have much greater reproductive success than can a female. When we recall that evolution is ultimately a question of some organisms leaving more descendants than others, we can begin to see a deep evolutionary foundation for one of the strangest findings of psychoanalysis and begin to understand why human females probably have good reason to envy their brothers the preference which they are usually shown. From this point of view, penis-envy would be the little girl's way of conceiving of what is, in reality, a much more abstract problem: her response to the evolutionary advantages of preferential parental investment in males.

Just why possession of the penis should be crucial is a matter to which we will return in a moment. For the time being, let us simply conclude that although envy of the penis may seem strange, the envy of males seems widely justified, especially considering the many privileges and advantages they are accorded, not merely within the family and in childhood, but in human cultures far and wide.

Yet our discussion of the positive side of the Oedipus complex should not blind us to its other aspects. My mention of the importance of the father should serve to remind us that if the little boy, for instance, is exploiting his affective relationship with his mother by use of suitably disguised sexual cues, then his father must be seen as a rival. After all, the mother's emotional and personal commitment has a finite value, and more for one male may mean correspondingly less for another. A father certainly can come to see his childern as competitors for his wife's affections and can harbour resentment against them; so it is not in the least surprising that boys can feel the same and come to see the father as a resented but feared rival, quite apart from their other, more positive attitudes towards him. We have only to add to this the characteristic tendency of children to think in emotional terms and to see things in black and white to find the death-wishes against the father which seem to typify the Oedipus complex of males. In a rather more complex way, and perhaps at a somewhat lower level of intensity as a result, comparable wishes might be expected in little girls.

To put the matter succinctly, we might say that, taking the more realistic view which sees child-development from the point of view of the child as well as from the conventional view of the parent, children can be expected to feel with regard to their parents in general but with regard to the same-sex parent in particular a notable, if uncon-scious, *ambivalence*. By this I mean that we can expect to find powerful feelings of love and hate directed at the same object. Since such contradictory feelings about one and the same person cause mental conflict, ambivalence is best made unconscious. Once repressed, the strong contradictory feelings which colour human relations with the parents constitute the core of the Oedipus complex and the latent content on which dreams, psychopathology and all kinds of manifest contents can draw. When we include in this picture the determinants of sexually ambiguous behaviour mentioned earlier we probably have most of the contributory components of most adult psycho-sexual conflict – the psychological core of neurosis and normality alike.

Resolution and identification

It not infrequently happens that a new way of looking at things reflects an insight into the conventional approach, which then appears in a quite different light, thanks to the new perspective. If we now return to the problem of the Oedipus complex and look at it from the point of view of the parents (and especially from that of the father) with the foregoing discussion in mind, we shall find what is perhaps the most impressive evidence for Freud's belief in its existence.

Fashionable modern social theories have claimed that the Oedipus complex is a product of Western – even middle-class Viennese – culture. In the case of the aborigines of central Australia little in the way of parental discipline is exercised during childhood. Children grow up to be notably spoilt and delinquent by Western standards because they are never consistently disciplined and are generally allowed to run wild. The two common 'traumas' connected with the oral and anal stages hardly occur because weaning is either very late by our standards or non-existent and because there is – or, rather, was in the traditional society – little effort to carry out toilet-training, which must have seemed un-necessary for a way of life spent entirely in the open.

Yet for all that a major trauma – which is a real trauma and has no need of quotation marks to qualify it – occurs at puberty. This is what is called *initiation*. It is a series of ceremonies carried out on boys who have entered ado-lescence. To these boys painful beatings and ordeals are administered by their clan 'fathers', prominent among whom will normally be the man who is going to be the boy's actual father-in-law. Such ceremonies usually culminate in circumcision or in some other comparable mutilation such as knocking out of teeth, pulling out of nails, scarification, or whatever. After successfully enduring these ordeals, the adolescent boys are then pronounced to be 'men'.

Although they may seem strange, rituals such as these are by no means without parallels in our own culture. Equivalents can be found in ordeals set for recruits to British public schools. North American university fraternities and sororities, crack military regiments, Masonic lodges, Hell's Angels chapters, and so on. All have one factor in common. By means of unpleasant, dangerous or humiliating ordeals they contrive to test the motivation of the recruits who want to be members of whatever the exclusive institution may be. They are tests of the degree to which aspiring members can identify with the values and traditions of the existing membership and prove that they are thereby fit to be members themselves.

In primitive hunter-gatherer societies like those of the aborigines of central Australia such tests are applied to all males who wish to be regarded as men. What the initiation ordeals test is the strength of the sons' identification with their fathers' values and traditions, among which sexual taboos related to incest and clan marriage laws are especially prominent. This almost certainly explains the universal popularity of circumcision because it seems that such genital mutilations as this (and this is not the only one practised) express the most fundamental aspect of the latent conflict between fathers and sons: the sexual one relating to the mother.

It seems as if initiation ritual in such societies provides a very definite trauma corresponding to the genital stage which begins at puberty and for which genital mutilations are therefore especially appropriate. The fuss that is usually made in such rituals about removing the boys from the protection of their mothers; the threats made against them in the name of the fathers; the beatings, punishments and humiliations which they collectively have to endure at their fathers' collective hands; the emphasis on the new responsibilities for sexual conduct which the newly initiated now carry – all these things add up to being a traumatic culmination of the Oedipus complex in which sons prove the strength of their identification with their fathers and the extent of their repression of the negative, hating, parricidal aspects of their own ambivalence. And if anyone doubts that this is a very real genital trauma, let me ask them how they would feel if, as a lad of fifteen or sixteen they had had to endure all this, along with the removal of their foreskin by hacking it off between two sharp stones or by some other traditionally palaeolithic method.

Nothing much like initiation happens in our societies, or, at least, not during adolescence. Circumcision does occur in some ethnic groups in early infancy, and some also have rites of passage for adolescent males, but, by and large and with these few significant exceptions, such genital traumas are unknown. However, Freud's finding was that in Western cultures there is indeed an equivalent trauma in childhood related, not to the final, definitive genital phase as in primitive societies which practise initiation rituals, but to the phallic, Oedipal period which precedes it.

Contrary to fashionable socialization theories which only take the point of view of the parents into account, children can deploy sexual and emotional tactics to obtain what they desire from the parents, especially the parent of the opposite sex, leading to the typical rivalry with the parent of the same sex. But the parents are not without weapons of their own in this conflict. They too can deploy effective tactics to counter the seductions of the child in the form of a general disapproval of infantile sexuality, a denial that they themselves ever behaved like that when they were young, numerous more or less disingenuous rationalizations, and the imposition of the incest-taboo.

This, effectively, is what we saw me doing during my breakfast-table discussion with my own son about why he could not marry his mother and which occasioned his classic Freudian slip of the tongue. Parents – and perhaps especially the parent of the same sex, since this is usually the one with most to lose in the situation – can counter infantile seduction in the interests of the child by sexual prohibitions in their own interests. This is also what primitive peoples do when they initiate their young men. In both instances the father sets a limit to the effectiveness of the son's emotional and sexual exploitation of the mother and demands evidence of the son's identification with him and his cultural values, among which the incest-taboo looms especially large and significant.

Although some primitive societies carry out initiation rituals on pubescent girls, sometimes with comparable genital and other mutilations, they are much less common than those carried out on boys and, in central Australia, notably absent. The reason for this may be the greater violence and clarity of the male Oedipus complex and its greater potential threat to the ' fathers; but another is probably the generally subservient role that women play in such societies. Largely controlled by the adult men, marriage soon after puberty marks the initiation of a woman, along with the birth of her first child. Furthermore, there may be good reasons for thinking that it is conflict between males over females which is critical for human societies, rather than female competition for men. However, the fundamental reason why female initiation and Oedipal resolution are perhaps more automatic and less marked by cultural rites probably lies in the castration complex, the subject to which we must now turn.

The castration complex

In cultures which do not have adolescent initiation the demand that the child should resolve its Oedipal ambivalence by identification with the values of the parents is often accompanied by both implicit and explicit threats of castration. The anthropologist and psychoanalyst Géza Róheim reports that, by contrast to central Australia where he never heard a castration-threat mentioned against a child and where adolescent initiation is the rule, in Melanesia where it is not, he noticed a popular 'game' during which fathers threaten to bite off the child's genitals! Freud reported that many of his patients had evidently been exposed to direct or indirect threats of castration, the latter contained in stories about masturbation causing blindness, insanity and so on.

In all of this the phallus plays a prominent symbolic role. This is what the little girl envies her brothers; this is what the son fears that the father will cut off; and it is a piece of this which the father does indeed cut off in the course of infantile or adolescent circumcision. The term *castration complex* covers these and many other manifestations of the phallus as a symbol in the complex unconscious code by means of which the libido expresses itself in the manifest content of the mind.

To understand why this is so, let us consider the place of language in mental topography. Because words are learnt and used at will, they obviously relate to the pre-conscious, that region of the mind from which the contents can be voluntarily recalled to consciousness. The sexual instinct, by contrast, arises in the unconscious region in which verbal representations, being pre-conscious, do not exist. Yet instincts need to gain admission to consciousness, at least to the extent that they must attempt to influence voluntary thought and action if they are to be satisfied in reality. In part this is achieved by subjective emotional or somatic sensations, such as salivation because of hunger, or feelings of love related to the sexual drive. But the latent contents of the unconscious can also register effects in consciousness by means of *symbolism*, by which I mean the use of pre-conscious ideas to represent latent, unconscious meanings.

An example of what I have in mind was provided earlier

by the little girl who gave up her wish to be a boy only to substitute a similar wish to be a giraffe. Analysis showed that it was the long neck of the giraffe which characterized it in her pre-conscious and that this idea in turn was influenced by an unconscious equation of the giraffe's neck with the human penis. It is by no means far-fetched to assume that in the unconscious, where linguistic terms and conscious thought are unknown, fundamental symbols are employed, borrowed from the pre-conscious because of their resemblance to simple, primitive, pre-verbal notions, such as that which represents the idea of maleness by reference to possession of the phallus.

Such symbolic simplicity should not surprise us, especially since we often encounter it in other areas where signs and symbols, rather than words, have to be employed. In road signs, for instance, abstract symbols and pictograms are routinely used to represent some quite complex ideas such as 'Do not overtake' or 'Give priority to traffic coming from the opposite direction'. If we imagine for a moment having to design a set of road signs related to sexual behaviour, I have little doubt that representations of the phallus would soon find a role and that images already familiar from dreams and psychopathology would become unavoidable. If we were not allowed the easy way out afforded by pictograms related to dress, we might even find that we had to represent a male as a figure with a penis, and a female as one without!

In short, we should expect the unconscious to deal in simple, basic symbols which have a direct and fundamental meaning and to represent the whole complex issue of male sexuality with one straightforward term: the physical reality of the penis. The charge sometimes made against Freud that his theory makes too much of the physical reality of the penis is, in this sense, perfectly justified. If it puts such an emphasis on the phallus, it is merely because the unconscious does so too.

Another consequence of the castration complex and one

of the weirdest findings of psychoanalytic investigations is illustrated once again by an anecdote about one of my own sons. At about the age of three he was with his mother while she was dusting a table-lamp. The lamp-stand in question represents a naked lady, holding up the light. When my wife removed the shade to dust the stand my son pointed up at the lady and laughingly said, 'Dat lady got no whistle – broken it!' A similar idea provides the joke in a sea-side postcard I once saw depicting a little boy and girl in the bath together. The little boy is looking at the little girl and saying, 'No, you can't play with mine. Look! you've already broken yours!'

Such assumptions are by no means uncommon. I can still vividly recall the first time I had an opportunity to inspect the genitals of a little girl. I was approximately six or seven years old, the girl slightly older. To this day I can recall seeing, not what was really there, a genital cleft, but its exact opposite – a strange, string-like penis which appeared to be glued to her body and which disappeared mysteriously as if she were hiding its end between her legs!

Looking back with the benefit of adult knowledge and hindsight I can clearly see what must have happened. Somehow my eyes (or, rather, my brain) played a trick on me similar to that intentionally exploited by psychologists or artists in drawing ambiguous figures which can be seen either as convex obtrusions or concave cavities, depending on one's assumption about the direction of the source of light. My eyes misinterpreted a concave cleft for a convex ridge by exploiting a similar ambiguity, with the result that I was sure that I had seen a penis – a strange one admittedly, but a penis of kinds nevertheless.

Again, at the age of about seven one of my sons overheard a conversation about the menopause. When asked to explain it, his mother did so, to which he replied: 'So I suppose they grow a penis after that!' Although myths abound attributing such attitudes to the influence of culture, it is significant that in the children's language of the Aranda aborigines of central Australia the word *mama* appears, as it does in the speech of our own children. But in the Aranda context it means, not 'Mother' but 'Mother's genital' and, apparently quite independently, 'wound'. These two meanings did not seem to be distinct in my son's mind when he reasoned – correctly, according to the castration complex – that, if a woman ceases bleeding from the wound which represents her genital, that wound could heal to the point of complete restoration – the re-appearance of the penis.

All these examples illustrate the view of the child which, contrary to parental and educational pressures, sees a woman as a castrated man. Perhaps this is because in the symbolic language of the unconscious the only way that the female can be represented is as a male deprived of his characteristic attribute – the phallus. In this symbolic language 'female' is indicated by the term 'not male' and 'not male' by 'no penis'. Furthermore, this is found to be a typical representation in the adult human unconscious and forms the latent basis of many strange sexual behaviours ranging from fetishism (where the fetish represents the missing female phallus) to aspects of transvestism and homosexuality, not to mention misogyny and the common belief of folk-lore that a woman could scare away the Devil by exposing her genitals (that is, by threatening him with castration)!

Like many of the findings of relativity, psychoanalytic investigations of the castration complex cannot but evoke a feeling of weirdness and perversity in the minds of most people, habituated as they must be to the pre-conscious, adult frame of reference. But, from the point of view of the young child and of the unconscious, it has a strange logic and bizarre beauty characteristically revealed in the delusions of psychotics. A final look at the Schreber case will illustrate what I mean.

Freud, looking at the material from Schreber's own psychological perspective, points out that his delusions began with characteristic fears of persecution at the hands of

Dr Flechsig, who Schreber believed would subject him to sexual abuse. Before long, this turned into a belief that God was the agent of a plot whose aim was to emasculate him and turn him into a woman. Schreber only began to improve when he realized that there was no stopping this process and that he had to submit obediently to such a transformation for 'a holy purpose' – the redemption of the world. Yet the designs of both God and Flechsig on him were clearly fundamentally the same, as is revealed by Schreber's references to 'God Flechsig'.

This delusion was elaborated to the point where on two separate occasions he believed that he had female genitals and that 'Nerves of God corresponding to male semen had, by a divine miracle, been projected into my body, and impregnation had thus taken place.' Such a mysterious experience was not unpleasant because feminization was evidently accompanied by considerable 'voluptuousness' caused by the infusion of female nerves.

Schreber's first, more positive relations with Flechsig at the time of the hypochondria (which provided the prelude to the illness) could hardly have given him grounds for suspecting that his doctor was a homicidal sexual pervert. But this only seems the case if we adopt the point of view of the pre-conscious, a frame of reference not privileged in psychoanalysis as far as the unconscious is concerned. If we examine it from the unconscious point of view it seems that a passive, masochistic wish could easily be accounted for as a relic of the Oedipal period of childhood, before Oedipal resolution fixes the sexual identity of a little boy.

Earlier we noticed two forms of masochism, erotogenic and moral. It would appear that Schreber's undoubted masochism had elements of both of these, related as it was both to physical sensations of 'voluptuousness' and to moral and psychological suffering at the hands of a God who did not understand human beings and could not learn from experience. But a third form of masochism also exists, what Freud termed the feminine form.

Feminine masochism arises out of the simple fact that the female sexual role is a largely passive, accepting one, as opposed to the aggressive, penetrating one of the male. The aggressive, castrating meaning which the castration complex attaches to it in childhood is retained in the frame of reference of the unconscious as a repressed, latent conviction that sexual intercourse amounts to castrating rape of the woman by the man. Such a latent attitude probably explains why female initiation is at best optional and really probably unnecessary: sexual intercourse for a woman is subjugation to the man, along with symbolic castration, like circumcision for a boy. In Schreber's delusions of emasculation it irrupts into consciousness in the form of a masochistic delusion. Its unmistakable reappearance in this form suggests that Schreber's hypochondria represented a process of narcissistic withdrawal by means of which his libido progressively retreated from later stages of development towards earlier, pre-genital ones.

Freud himself was fond of using the analogy of an occupying army, which leaves garrisons at towns along the line of its advance, to illustrate the process of libidinal maturity and the possibility of regression. The libido may advance like such an army, but, like it, it leaves residues at fixation points along the way. A major defeat can lead to retreat to the earlier outposts, as the returning forces seek refuge in previously secure positions.

In a similar way, Schreber's libido seems to have regressed along the developmental line which leads from auto-eroticism to Oedipal resolution and genital primacy. Freud speculates that it may have been disappointment in not having children of his own, plus the temporary absence of his wife, which triggered the retreat under pressure of work. Once begun it gathered momentum alarmingly. From the genital stage which he had presumably reached in his relations with his wife, Schreber regressed to Oedipal conflict represented by his extreme ambivalence, first about Flechsig, and then about God.

Whereas hysteria condenses latent content into symptoms, paranoias like that of Schreber decompose latent content into various parts which then appear as manifest symptoms. His delusions about emasculation reflect passive, homosexual attachments to the father represented as a feminine, masochistic self-prostration to the impregnating 'rays of God'. This reappearance of a passive, homosexual relation to the father suggests regression to a state before Oedipal resolution. At this point my earlier mention of Schreber's pleasurable anal sensations becomes immediately comprehensible because the anus is an anatomical equivalent of the female genital and plays the passive, accepting role of that organ in male homosexuality. But the fact that Schreber believed that he had to be transformed into a woman in the course of this regression demonstrates that, in the reference system of the unconscious, the castration complex determines latent equations of masculinity with activity and the phallus, and feminity with passiveness and castration.

In Freud's view the consequence of the castration complex was to force children to repress their incestuous interest in the parent of the opposite sex and instead to identify with the parent of the same sex. By doing this the boy saved his own penis from the threat of castration and imagined that he possessed that of his father, so much more impressive than his own. Correspondingly, the little girl accepted her subjectively felt, but repressed feeling of being already castrated and identified with her mother who had suffered a fate like herself, but who possessed compensations suggested by the castration complex: the father who bore the penis, and the baby which could be a substitute for it. But whatever the weird details of the libidinal symbolism – and anyone who examines human sexual life soon learns that it is weird indeed – the overall psychological situation seems clear: the child is forced to resolve its infantile ambivalance by means of identification with the parents and their values.

Where this process does not occur in this way apparent sexual abnormalities appear. For instance, a boy who cannot bring himself to identify with his father may instead do so with his mother and become a passive homosexual seeking to play his mother's role as he perceived it in childhood, rather than his father's. Again, a woman may so resent the implication of her unconscious that she is a castrated man that she may harbour a life-long resentment and antagonism towards the opposite sex. The consequence is that there must be, from the psychological point of view, at least four sexes: apart from masculine males and feminine females we must also expect feminine males and masculine females – those whose Oedipal resolutions are based on identification with the cross-sex parent. In reality, the variations are endless and the possible outcomes complex indeed. An introductory chapter like this one cannot possibly go into even a fraction of them; but, for the time being, let me conclude with the following observation.

As we saw, Freud initially believed that most adult psychopathology was caused by traumatic seduction during infancy. The use of the free association method soon showed that this was too simple and crude a view. It showed that children were not the passive victims of adult libidos but had libidinal motives of their own which gave rise to profound ambivalence in their relations with their parents and parental surrogates. His final view, embodied in the mature libido theory and the idea of the Oedipus complex, both retained the earlier seduction theory and reversed it. Now the universal traumas originated not in seduction of children by adults, but in adults' attempts to restrain the libidinal development of children by means of weaning, toilet-training and, above all, proscription of infantile sexuality in general and prescription of the incest-taboo in particular.

Whilst never denying that adult seduction of children could or did occur, it turned out that, as far as a proper understanding of normal human sexual development was concerned, it was not so much adults who seduced children as children who attempted to seduce adults in order to procure the extensive parental care on which the human child has come to rely. In this sense the modern view of the Oedipus complex is the seduction theory turned on its head, with subject and object transposed and the overt victimization of the one turned into the implicit exploitation of the other.

6

The Second Psychoanalytic Revolution

The Gross method of psychoanalysis

The adoption of the definitive version of the libido theory with its emphasis on the active, precocious sexual life of the child and the central crisis of the Oedipus complex was not the only direction in which Freud's thinking developed after his disillusionment with the seduction theory. In the early 1920s a new picture of the mind began to emerge, represented in the famous id–ego–superego model. However, the adoption of this so-called *second topography* affected much more than just psychoanalytic theory. It was profoundly involved in psychoanalytic treatment itself, was ultimately to make the psychoanalysis of children possible, and was to lead to a notable shift in emphasis which corresponded not only to new theoretical and therapeutic trends, but to new social and cultural ones as well.

Much confusion exists because people fail to appreciate the extent and significance of the post-1920 developments and so, in order to highlight the distinction as dramatically as possible, I propose to introduce the subject by means of a recently published account of an early psychoanalytic cure by one of Freud's most colourful and extraordinary followers.

The account from which I wish to quote is contained in a letter written in 1907 to Freud by Erich Mühsam, described as 'a well-known litterateur and anarchist', who was treated by Otto Gross (1847–1915) who held the post of *Dozent* in psychiatry at the University of Graz. For a while, and despite his life-long addiction to drugs, Gross 'came to be considered by many as Freud's most eminent follower'.★

Freud's biographer and early colleague, Ernest Jones (1879-1958) saw him as 'the nearest approach to the romantic ideal of a genius I have ever met', and describes his 'unorthodox' technique of carrying out analytic treatments at a café table! Gross appears to have possessed a power of divining the thoughts of others which was quite unparalleled, and combined this unusual talent with an astonishing revolutionary and anarchistic ideology which saw the cause of all psychological and cultural problems in bourgeois patriarchy and the solution in anarchistic matriarchy. According to Jung's account, Gross believed that 'the truly healthy state for the neurotic is sexual immorality' and he and his followers indulged in wild orgies designed to demonstrate their own liberation from conventional morals.

Today such a person as Gross would not be allowed near a psychoanalytic institute, let alone become a member, yet Mühsam's unsolicited letter to Freud proves that Gross, despite his crude approach and narrow cathartic method, could nevertheless achieve therapeutic results in the space of a few weeks which today would seem miraculous after a much longer period.

Mühsam introduces himself to Freud saying that he hopes 'the report of a patient on an exceedingly successful cathartic treatment may have sufficient interest . . . to excuse this letter'. He then lists his symptoms. According to his account he suffered from 'a severe hysteria' involving acute neurotic irritability, 'outbreaks of rage', 'twilight states' with partial sensory and motor paralysis, sometimes culminating in transitory hysterical blindness and complete

★All the references in this chapter to the Mühsam case come from K. R. Eissler, *Victor Tausk's Suicide* (New York, 1983) and the translation of Mühsam's letter by Ruth Eissler contained in the appendix, quoted by kind permission.

sensory disorientation. He states that he was cured of these disabling symptoms after a mere six weeks of treatment. Assuming that Gross followed contemporary analytic practice, this would have meant six one-hour sessions a week – whether or not in the café he does not say, I think probably not – or, in other words, 36 hours of therapy!

In the next paragraph of his letter he gives a partial explanation of the extraordinary speed and effectiveness of the treatment, even by the standards of the day. He says that his literary gifts enabled him to free associate rapidly and easily, and he gives a classic account of catharsis when he observes: 'The dawning ability to lead the symptoms of my illness back to their deeper foundations brought about, more and more, the disappearance of those very symptoms, and I was able to observe how sometimes through a question of the physician and the consequent answer with its associations, suddenly an entire crust of the disease fell off.' He adds that even outside the therapeutic situation the process continued quite spontaneously.

Mühsam shows a profound understanding of the therapeutic aims of psychoanalysis when he says that he 'found its value especially in the fact that the task of the physician would be mainly to make the patient himself the physician. The patient is induced to diagnose his sickness. On the basis of the diagnosis discovered by himself, he . . . carries out his own cure. He is brought to the point where he is no longer interested in himself as a sufferer but in the suffering itself. He objectifies his condition. He does not put the importance anymore upon himself as a pitiable patient, as the emotionally martyred, as a hysteric seeking cure, but as a physician . . . This transformation of the subjective sensations into objective values is the process of the cure.'

Finally, he voices a common misgiving about psychoanalysis in saying that he 'had feared lest the treatment might paralyse my productivity as a lyricist' but adds that 'Today I may state with pleasure that this apprehension did not come true. To the contrary: by the removal of numerous interfering phenomena which had laid themselves around the core of my being, my psyche has become more sensitive and reacts more easily to influences which stimulate artistic productivity.' He concludes the letter with a tribute to Gross's skill, tact and consideration and with a further one to Freud's psychology, which he feels is that 'of a genius'.

The transference neurosis

In a book published in 1920 Freud commented that in the beginning psychoanalysis 'could do no more than discover the unconscious material that was concealed from the patient, put it together, and, at the right moment, communicate it to him. Psychoanalysis was then first and foremost an art of interpreting.'* It was one, evidently, in which characters like Gross excelled. But Freud goes on to point out that this technique, successful as it apparently was in cases like Mühsam's, proved of limited effectiveness. He comments that it soon became clear that such interpretations needed to be confirmed by the patient's own memory and that the analytic task shifted its focus slightly to include the resistances which attempted to keep the repressed material unconscious. Had this not been so, psychoanalysts would have found that cures like that reported by Mühsam were commonplace and that a few weeks of intensive interpretation would cure any neurosis.

Unfortunately psychoanalysis, not to mention the human mind, is not so simple. Resistance proved difficult to overcome simply by intellectual means – merely telling patients what was wrong with them and why was no good. The analyst needed to overcome the patient's inner,

---

*S. Freud, *Beyond the Pleasure Principle, Standard Edition of the Complete Psychological Works of Sigmund Freud* (London, 1953–1974) vol. XVIII, p. 18.

emotional resistance to uncovering the unconscious which was primarily of an irrational and emotional nature and ultimately served the interests of the pleasure principle. Resistance exists in order to prevent the conscious mind from becoming painfully aware of some unpleasant mental conflict. We saw in my typewriter example that resistance expressed itself as an inability to remember about the ribbon-feed control and its effects but that after the occasion for the conflict had passed the resistance relented, and the repressed returned to consciousness.

Since most neurotics are suffering from on-going and much more profound mental conflicts than that which afflicted me on the Bank Holiday weekend over my typing, it follows that resistance cannot be expected to be so accommodating. A chronic conflict creates chronic resistance against it: consciousness would rather not be bothered by it and so sets up effective barriers against anything which might call it to mind. The analyst tries to get the patient to recall it, but, in doing so, encounters the force of resistance as an unwillingness to accept the analytic interpretations and to recognize the unconcious conflict as it becomes visible. Freud's first response to this difficult situation was to use the important phenomenon of *transference* as an ally in the fight.

Transference is certainly one of the strangest and, until recently, one of the most inexplicable findings of psychoanalysis. According to what most people know, it amounts to the patient being in love with the analyst. Whilst this can certainly be one aspect of it, transference is a much wider and more profound phenomenon. Essentially it consists in the tendency of the unconscious to interpret present experiences and relationships as repetitions of earlier ones – usually as repetitions of childhood. As a consequence, transference is by no means something confined to the analytic situation, as the following example indicates.

Not long before writing this book I was looking back through an old diary and suddenly came across a startling fact. At the time of her death some years ago, I was undergoing a didactic analysis with Anna Freud. Until finding the diary, I had the distinct and unmistakable recollection that my last visit to her had been in hospital. Now I discovered objective and irrefutable proof that it had not been. It seemed that, in the space of a mere two or three years of the actual event, I had transposed the dates of two visits, one to her home, which had been the last time I actually saw her, and an earlier one to the hospital.

Why had this astonishing transposition occurred? Transference easily explained it. The last time I had seen my mother had been in hospital, when I was 4 years old. My father had prevented me from going to see her for the last few weeks before she died there. On my visit to Anna Freud in the hospital I had been prevented from seeing her (despite having the approval of the hospital authorities) by her own doctor, who stood guard in the room. Evidently my analytic transference to Anna Freud as representing my mother, so obvious in the analysis, had reasserted itself here after her death and made my memory reconstruct the order of my final visits to her on the pattern of my earlier memories of my mother's last illness.

In the clinical situation such a tendency to unconsciously reconstruct a new situation on the basis of an infantile one routinely leads to the analyst being seen as a parental figure, either father or mother as the case may be (a tendency understandably encouraged if, as is not unusually the case, the analyst is of the right relative age to the patient). Analytic investigations of hypnosis showed that here too the effect of the hypnotist depended on the patient seeing the therapist as a parental authority figure, one who was qualified to 'put the patient to sleep' and take over responsibility for consciousness.

Just as hypnosis had given way to the pressure method of suggestion, so pure free association and interpretation gave way to suggestion operating as transference in the sense that the analyst found that he could use the positive parental role as one which reinforced the authority of his interpretations. This stage of the development of analysis, which was actually quite a short one and was over (in Freud's case at least) well before World War I, is important because popular understanding has remained fixated at this point and still persists in thinking of transference only in terms of the analyst's suggestive powers over the patient.

Yet this too turned out to be inadequate and was, in any case, counter to the spirit of psychoanalysis. Analysis, as opposed to suggestion, consists in overcoming symptoms through objective insight rather than uncomprehending positive transferences to the person of the analyst. The problem was that, even with the use of suggestion, the patient could not usually be encouraged to remember everything and so lacked ultimate conviction of the truth of the analyst's interpretations. Here another astonishing aspect of transference came to the rescue when it became apparent that patients could not merely be induced to remember but that they usually began spontaneously and compulsively to *act out* the transference in the course of the analysis.

Acting out can take almost any form and is usually typified by being compulsive and embarrassingly unsuited to the objective aspects of the analytic situation. Yet this makes it all the easier to interpret and means that such interpretations carry tremendous conviction with patients once they can bring themselves to admit the compulsive nature of their behaviour. In short, what we have is a *transference neurosis* – a situation in which patients recreate important aspects of their original neurosis in the new conditions of the analysis.

The transference neurosis is a kind of artificially induced neurotic disturbance which represents a contemporaneous recapitulation of the past, a return of the repressed which carries the analysand, so to speak, back with it to the time in which the original conflict situation occurred. Not surprisingly, it is invariably found that the period to which the transference neurosis preferentially returns is that of the

Oedipus complex and its derivatives and parallels. In the transference neurosis such a return to the Oedipal period carries with it the possibility of retrospectively correcting the past by resolving the neurosis in the present.

This makes the mature psychoanalytic method rather different from the early cathartic one and explains why the latter could appeal so much to an anarchist and revolutionary like Gross. According to Jung, 'Dr Gross tells me that he puts a quick stop to the transference by turning people into sexual immoralists. He says the transference to the analyst and its persistent fixation are mere monogamy symbols and as such symptoms of repression.'

In a sense, Gross was right. As we have seen, the transference neurosis is a symptom of repression in the sense that no neurosis can exist without chronic irresolution of the conflict which underlies it. Yet Gross was a little hasty in dismissing it as useless to the analyst. What Freud believed, but what Gross did not, was that the aim of analysis was not to unleash the instinctual drives of patients by turning them from repressed into active perverts, but to enable them to resolve their conflicts with their own instinctual drives and to replace unconscious, automatic repression ultimately in the service of the pleasure principle with conscious, rational renunciation in the interests of reality.

According to Freud, successful analysis led via the Oedipus complex to conscious mastery of the unconscious, not to surrender to it. For him, unlike Gross, the undoing of repressions was not the end of analysis, only the beginning. Its aim was the attainment of mastery over what had been repressed, not mere catharsis. According to Freud, neurotics were not so much repressed perverts as normal human beings temporarily overwhelmed by neurotic conflicts which they could not master. Psychoanalysis was a means of reawakening that moral courage to face reality which we could hardly be expected to have possessed as children, but which, as adults, we so badly need.

The ego and the id

In the first, predominantly cathartic, period of psycho-analysis, the unconscious was envisaged as a kind of dammed-up torrent of primeval instinctual energies, strain-ing to break through the barrier of consciousness to expression and satisfaction. Some early analysts like Gross believed that the aim of analysis was to open the flood-gates, and later members of the same tradition like Wilhelm Reich glorified the orgasm as the touchstone of normality and mental health. Today, much popular opinion still sees psychoanalysis from this rather outdated point of view.

The reason that it is outdated is that, by about 1920, a second and much more sophisticated model of the mind had begun to emerge. Now things were seen from the point of view of the *ego*, understood as the partly conscious, but mainly unconscious, agency of the personality responsible for voluntary movement, thought and intention. According to the new way of looking at things it faced demands upon it from three different origins.

First came internal demands from its unconscious instinc-tual drives and other repressed elements, now seen as a separate agency called the *id*. The id was an impersonal, chaotic inferno of primal drives and dynamically repressed material which constantly agitated for expression. It com-municated with the ego through subjective somatic inner-vations (like salivation associated with hunger or erection associated with sexual arousal), and via emotional, intuitive and pre-verbal thought. It goaded the ego with pain and seduced it with pleasure; if its demands went unsatisfied in any significant way and the ego had no other means of defending itself against them it felt *neurotic anxiety* as a result. To safeguard itself the ego deployed various defence measures against the id, much the most important of which was repression.

Secondly came demands from reality, directed into the

ego by the perceptual system and reinforced by memory. If the functioning of the ego with regard to the id was dominated by the pleasure principle, then in its relations with perception the reality principle held sway. The ego found that it had to take the demands of the latter seriously into account in deliberating how to execute its responsibilities for voluntary movement and thought. Failure to meet the demands of reality led to the ego experiencing *realistic anxiety.*

Finally, the ego was faced with demands originating in the so-called *superego*, a specialized subdivision of itself which was based on identification and internalization of the more competent, dominant egos which the child found around itself. In the main, the superego took on its definitive form with the resolution of the Oedipus complex, involving an identification of the child with the values and ideals of the parents. Consequently, the superego provided a sense of moral and aesthetic self-judgement (conscience and values, in other words), both in a positive sense as acting as an *ego-ideal* and in the negative one in performing the role of censor of the ego's wishes. It also provided much of the ego's sense of reality because the latter had had to learn much about the world not merely by direct experience, but from the parents and their equivalents in childhood. Failure to meet the demands of the superego created a feeling of *moral anxiety.*

In a new and much more subtle classification of psychopathology it now became clear that conflicts between the ego and the id were likely to take the form of hysteria or obsessional neurosis and that in both cases the core of the disorder was likely to be an unconscious and unresolved conflict between the defence mechanisms of the ego and the drives of the id. The symptoms of the disorder represented unsuccessful attempts by the repressed to return to consciousness; the ego's defences being seen as partially successful attempts to prevent them from doing so.

Conflicts between the ego and reality were likely to

constitute *psychoses* such as paranoia and schizophrenia, both of which involved disturbances in the ego's grasp on the real world, something further compromised by the ego's defensive withdrawal from the realities which threatened it. In these cases symptoms were mainly to be seen as unsuccessful attempts by the ego to regain lost libidinal ties with outside objects.

Finally, conflict between the ego and superego could give rise to *manic-depressive disorders* in which the ego became disturbed in its relationship with itself, its identifications and projections. Psychoanalysis was most suitable for the first category of conflicts between the ego and the id because such conflicts readily lent themselves to forming transference neuroses in analysis. It was found to be less effective in treating manic-depressive disorders, and almost useless in the case of psychoses. In the case of manic-depressive disorders this was mainly because the central conflict is confined within the ego and unamenable to externalization in the transference. In the case of the psychoses the ego seems already to have been overwhelmed by a conflict which undermines the reality of which the analysis itself is part.

As far as normal psychology was concerned, Freud pointed out that character could be classified on the basis of which agency was uppermost. He termed the character in which the id and its needs took first place the *erotic*, and saw it as dominated by the need to be loved. That in which the ego was dominant he termed the *narcissistic* character-type and saw it as more independent and mainly concerned with the individual's own self-preservation. Finally, the personality characterized by the superego he termed *obsessional*. This type exhibited great self-reliance because it took more account of its own conscience than its need to be loved by others and became the pre-eminent vehicle of cultural values. He expressed the view that the erotic type was more likely to suffer from hysteria, thanks to the prominence in that type of the id and its needs; while the narcissistic type was correspondingly predisposed to psychosis, because of the pre-eminence of the ego. Inevitably, the obsessional character was most likely to develop an obsessional neurosis.

More numerous than the pure types were the mixed: the *narcissistic-erotic* being very common, and something of a unity of opposites, with both self-preservative and other-directed instincts coming together. In the case of the *obsessional-erotic* the need to be loved relates mainly to parental surrogates and restricts the demands of the id with the censorship of the superego. The *narcissistic-obsessional* type was the one which Freud regarded as most valuable from the cultural point of view, combining the self-sufficiency of the ego-dominated narcissistic type with the cultural values of the obsessional. Finally, an *erotic-obsessional-narcissistic* combination was also in theory possible, but this would correspond to ideal normality, being a nicely balanced synthesis of all three agencies.

Although Freud never put the matter in this way, one might add that it is possible to see the various solutions to psychological conflicts in terms of which agency predominates in them. For instance, one could say that an *id-resolution* was one in which instinctual drives found satisfaction by some means and thereby resolved the conflict.

A typical example would be a perversion, and we have already seen that this was the type of resolution of neurotic conflict favoured by Gross. It also seems to have been the solution hit upon by Schreber, whose psychosis resulted from conflicts relating to passiveness and femininity and was eventually resolved to some extent by his adopting the perverse practice of transvestism as a gratification of his feminine instinctual trends. Such resolutions would presumably be more likely in the erotic type.

By contrast to this, one might also envisage a *superego-resolution:* one in which the conflict is resolved by the ego submitting to the superego's demands. Prime examples might be religious conversion, or some kind of identification with a cultural ideology where it is the values and ideals of the superego which prescribe the resolution of the conflict.

Whereas id-resolutions are always gratifications of instinct, superego-solutions usually take the form of *sublimations* (in other words, instinctual gratifications deprived of their original aim and supplied with another, culturally-approved one) or identifications, usually with parental-surrogates. Inevitably, they can be expected in persons of the obsessional type.

Finally, a possibility exists that a psychological conflict could result in an *ego-resolution*. The two previous types of resolution, along with psychopathology in general, would correspond to unconscious, aborted ego-resolutions, attempts by the ego to master an internal conflict which fail. Alternatively, they can be seen as ego-resolutions which fail because they obey the pleasure principle, rather than attempt to resolve a conflict by making a choice dictated by reality.

Here any kind of rational decision which meets the demands of reality would be an instance, but the best example of the successful ego-resolution would be the ideal analytic cure. This would correspond to Freud's concept of what psychoanalysis was all about: a realistic, conscious solution to a psychological conflict voluntarily brought about by an ego which had emancipated itself from enslavement to the id or compulsive obedience to the superego.

Ego-analysis and child-therapy

In the period before World War I psychoanalysis was mainly id-analysis in that it limited itself to discovering the repressed and then achieving catharsis by abreaction – that is, expressing the conflict along with the emotions involved. If I might use one of those archaeological metaphors so beloved by Freud himself (although this one was actually suggested to me by Anna Freud), early psychoanalysis was like early archaeology – a raid on the buried treasures of the mind directed at recovering objects of maximum value in the minimum time. After World War I ego-analysis developed rather as modern, scientific archaeology did, that is, as a careful, layer-by-layer clearance of the whole site which took into account everything found, the defences of the ego as well as the repressions hidden in the id.

Now psychoanalysis became something much more like a dissection of the total personality; not merely the uncovering of the id, but the analysis of the ego as well. Instead of pursuing free associations to discover the hidden contents of the repressed unconscious, the analyst could approach the ego itself and examine its various defence mechanisms as indicative of its basic structure.

One welcome by-product of defence-analysis was that for the first time reliable analysis of children became possible. Previously it had been impossible because children cannot free associate in the classical manner and because they almost invariably come to analysis against their will, so that they lack the motivation of adults (which is usually to get over some problem in their professional or love life). However, once mechanisms of defence became explicable in themselves child analysis was possible because the analyst could now observe these in the child and in reports from parents, teachers and others.

For instance, a child who, shall we say, exhibited independence and self-reliance to an abnormal degree, perhaps to the point of being unable to form any real relationships with others, might be suspected of building defences against a catastrophic object-loss in the past. Here the exaggerated degree of self-reliance belies the exact opposite in the unconscious and suggests an immature ego trying to be prematurely independent and self-contained because it is still so dependent on the object that has been lost.

Such an approach as this led directly to Anna Freud's

diagnostic profile, a formal evaluation of the status of a child's progress along a number of *developmental lines* related both to analysis of defences and to general evaluation of psycho-sexual maturity. Examples might be the prime libidinal developmental line from *auto-eroticism to genital dominance* along which we saw Schreber regressing, or that from *total dependency to self-reliance*, from *suckling to rational eating*, or from *infantile egocentricity to adult sociability*.

Contrary to the static perspectives of other views of child-development, the modern Freudian view appreciates that children do not advance along all developmental lines at an equal rate or to an equal extent. (One practical application of this is that Anna Freud usually advised parents of gifted children not to send them to special schools to further exaggerate the inherent discrepancy between the child's development along the intellectual/cognitive line as opposed to others such as the psycho-sexual.) Having established the child's developmental profile in terms of progress relative to the various dimensions, the child analyst could evaluate much more objectively the true nature of the underlying problem.

Another consequence of the shift from id- to ego-analysis was that analytic treatments now began to take very much longer. Whereas, as we saw in the Mühsam case, id-analyses could be completed in months – even in weeks in that case – ego-analyses, like modern, scientific archaeological digs, usually take years. Yet this cost also conveys a very real benefit, because now analysis can cover much more ground and reveal very much more about the personality than was ever possible in the early, cathartic days. This is thanks to the fact that defence-analysis includes not merely the uncovering of the repressed id, but the analysis of the unconscious ego, its transferences, defences and internal structure.

Looking at the matter in terms of id-, ego- and superego-resolutions, one might say that hypnosis and the early use of positive transference to overcome resistance approximated to more of a superego-resolution than anything else because the therapist exploited the role of the parent in the transference to urge the ego to overcome its timidity and come to terms with the conflict. But, with the adoption of the mature psychoanalytic method of defence-analysis, the analyst could give up this role and instead concentrate attention on freeing the ego of the patient from its encumbering defences and thereby allow it to resolve its conflicts without them. In terms of our resolution-schema, analysis had reached its definitive aim: ego-resolution of internal conflict made possible by the analysis of the ego's defences.

Inevitably in this process, the Oedipal period has to be revisited because this stage of development usually closes with something of a superego-solution of the Oedipal crisis, whereby the immature ego defends itself from the Oedipal conflict by means of identification with the parents and their values. In the analysis of the transference neurosis this if-you-can't-beat-them-join-them tactic has to be revisited so that a mature ego-resolution can occur. Instead of automatic and unknowing repression of incestuous wishes, the ego can attempt a conscious resolution of the Oedipal dilemma by means of the analysis of the transference to the person of the analyst. Consequently, transference-analysis is the prime method of modern psychoanalysis and the touch-stone of its authenticity.

Let me illustrate the essential added dimension which ego-analysis has brought by concluding this chapter with brief accounts of two modern case histories which will serve to highlight the contrast with the id-analytic methods of early followers of psychoanalysis like Gross.

The cases which I want to mention briefly were described in a remarkable article published in 1970 by two New York analysts. Both patients were young people brought up in the then-fashionable 'permissive' atmosphere and both cases illustrate the shortcomings of the earlier cathartic approach in the modern social climate.*

The first case concerns a girl who entered analysis at 14 and had been diagnosed as schizophrenic. Her analyst commented that her development had been distorted by her parents' permissiveness and their excessive identification with the child's drives. Her symptoms were feelings of alienation, frustration and indefinable – in other words, unconscious – guilt. Her parents, evidently sophisticated and superficially acquainted with psychoanalysis, felt unable to restrain her precocious sexual activities because of ambivalence about their own feelings and uneasiness lest they should be motivated by jealousy.

A period of promiscuity was followed by an unsatisfactory but apparently compulsive relationship with a young man who was homosexual and who committed suicide. There followed an unsuccessful marriage and a period of total promiscuity, often with the dregs of society, her dropout from higher education, with mounting depression and fear at her own self-destructiveness. Analysis revealed unresolved Oedipal conflicts which might once have resulted in hysteria, but which, in the permissive climate of the times, led to unrestrained and self-destructive acting out.

Essentially, we might say that the young woman in question was implicitly trying to achieve an id-resolution like that favoured by Gross, but failing miserably. Because her ego was weak and unsupported by her superego or her parents, her wild behaviour was not liberating but self-destructive. There was nothing in principle at fault with her id: it was her ego which was pathologically unable to cope with the demands placed upon it. Unlike those who reach successful id-resolutions, she could not establish a relationship which would allow her to gratify her perverse feelings in a stable and effective way. Because her behaviour was

*H. and Y. Lowenfeld, 'Our Permissive Society and the Superego', *The Psychoanalytic Quarterly*, vol. 39 (1970), pp. 590–608. For a further discussion see C. Badcock, *Madness and Modernity* (Oxford, 1983), chs. 3 and 5.

basically self-destructive, it could not lead to a resolution of the conflict, only to an expression and an exaggeration of it.

The second case is of a boy referred for treatment at the age of 12 because of school-phobia, self-damaging behaviour, fear and guilt. Analysis revealed the reason to have been incest with an elder sister. When the sister left home he began to cling to his mother and to manifest infantile behaviour. The permissive and over-indulgent father gave the boy no support to cope with his drives and sadistic fantasies. Like the previous case, he became increasingly paralysed by guilt and anxiety.

Unlike our first example, this one attempted something of a superego-solution in joining a Communist youth group and showed the expected improvement. However, unfortunately for him, his father confessed to being a Communist himself and he soon exchanged the party badge for a series of obscene ones. Like the first case, this one showed evidence of a weak ego, unsupportive superego and uncontrollable drives.

In a manner which would probably have surprised early id-analysts like Gross, experience has taught that liberation of the child's id merely creates new problems for the immature ego which, no longer subject to guilt and anxiety from the superego which has largely abdicated, instead feels only fear and apprehension aroused by its own uncontrollable drives. Contrary to the case of individuals like Gross, whose protest, anarchism and anti-moralism were probably designed to defend the id from an over-developed superego and which certainly developed in a social climate of emphatic moral values and secure cultural ideals, the more recent permissive moral climate has created conditions where such solutions to psychological conflict are likely to be increasingly unsuccessful. The fundamental reason is that they afflict the ego and the superego rather than the id and, as such, pose problems insoluble to the narrow, cathartic id-analysis of the first period of psychoanalysis. But once the mature id–ego–superego model, along with modern ego-analysis had emerged, pathology of the ego could, in principle, be as readily confronted as that of the id had been in the first, heroic period before World War I.

Furthermore, the whole question of the interrelation between the individual ego and the wider society could come under analytic scrutiny, especially since, partly thanks to psychoanalysis itself, social conditions changed dramatically from those in which collective values and the cultural superego could be taken for granted to those in which they most certainly could not. Such considerations bring us directly to the subject of our next two chapters, namely the social dimension of Freud's thought and the plight of psychoanalysis in the modern world.

7

Mass Psychology

The ambivalence of thoughts

In part, the Oedipus complex relates to impossible desires of impossible situations. While the son or daughter is a child adult sexual relations with the parent of the opposite sex is an obvious impossibility; and the possibilities of such a future relationship when the child has grown up are naturally limited by the discrepancy in age between parents and children. But only to a point; to a much larger extent the possibility of incest is constrained not by such natural factors but by an apparently arbitrary one – the incest-taboo.

Much of the psychological conflict relating to the Oedipus complex originates in the fact that Oedipal wishes are more or less totally under the influence of the pleasure principle and have no chance of realization, along with subsequent modification, by the reality principle. Permanently insulated from reality by repression, incestuous wishes can luxuriate in the unconscious, unaffected by facts, experience or conscious intention. They represent a problem 'swept under the carpet' of consciousness, so to speak.

But where do the incest-taboos originate? Surely the argument here is circular: the incest-taboo makes Oedipal wishes unrealizable; the impossibility of the Oedipal wishes makes the incest-taboo inevitable, and so on. At the very least, we might wonder why incest has to be tabooed and where this strange limitation on human sexual life came from. Freud's answer is contained in a remarkable work published in 1913, entitled *Totem and Taboo*.

Then, as today, two principal rival theories of incest-avoidance existed. It was and is still thought by some that the avoidance of incest is 'natural' in the sense that people have some kind of inner, automatic, perhaps genetic mechanism which makes them averse to sexual relations with members of their immediate family. The main difficulty with this theory – apart from an almost total lack of factual evidence in its favour and overwhelming evidence against it – is that if incest-avoidance is 'natural' in this sense then why bother to have elaborate taboos, laws and avoidances to prevent it? Surely people do not have to be prevented by such means from doing things which they do not want to do anyway? This theory may think that it can explain incest-avoidance, but it can hardly hope to explain the existence of the taboo.

A second theory is the exact opposite: it sees incest-avoidance as purely cultural and 'arbitrary'. According to this point of view, people would commit incest if they could but are prevented from doing so by taboos which have valuable social functions, such as the creation of kin relations and other aspects of culture. This explains the taboo, but not why it should relate to incest.

Freud's theory was quite different. He accounted for both the taboo and the importance of incest by suggesting that each stood for one side of a fundamental ambivalence – in this case both a desire to commit incest and an opposing one not to do so.

He pointed out that cultural taboos are very much reminiscent of *neurotic prohibitions*, which are a kind of personal taboo. An example might be the case mentioned earlier of the woman who could not bring herself to walk down a certain street in Vienna. This was because of a fundamental conflict relating to death-wishes against her husband represented by a shop bearing his name right next to an undertaker's. The desire to avoid and repress the whole unpleasant conflict led to a fear of being reminded of it by this accidental circumstance and a subsequent avoidance of the street in question. This seems closely analogous to taboos about visiting certain locations which are common, for instance, among the Australian aborigines. In the case of the Viennese lady personal ambivalence about her husband underlay her personal taboo on the street in question; in the case of cultural incest-taboos Freud believed that collective ambivalence about incest sustained them in an exactly similar way.

But incest is not the only tabooed subject one can find. In primitive societies Freud showed that taboos relating to the treatment of enemies, rulers and the dead could all be shown to reflect fundamental ambivalence towards each category of person. For instance, ceremonies carried out among primitive peoples for slain enemies suggest the presence of positive as well as negative feelings and of remorse, guilt and fear as well as hatred, exultation and triumph. Similarly, not every response to rulers is positive in its emotional origin. Freud points out that the ceremonial taboos on kings (such things as never allowing their feet to touch the ground or their persons to come into contact with anything tabooed to them) in fact impose severe restraints on their freedom and comfort which can be seen as revenge for their privileges. Again, treatment of the dead in all societies reflects not merely loving, sorrowful reactions, but also fearful, guilt-ridden and hating ones as well.

All of these taboos, like personal neurotic prohibitions, exist because the emotional ambivalence in question remains in the unconscious and has to be safeguarded against by the prohibition in question. But it is the pleasure principle, and not reality, which presides in the unconscious and one of its most notable and troublesome attributes is to promote what in the words of one of Freud's patients became known as the *omnipotence of thoughts*.

Our Viennese lady with the street-taboo will illustrate the

point. What harm, we might ask, is there in just walking down a street, even if it does remind one of death-wishes against one's husband? Surely this is not really a danger? After all, a wish is a wish, not an act. Perhaps so. But this is because we are speaking about it from the viewpoint of the conscious mind, presided over, in this case, by the reality principle. In reality wishes are distinct from acts, but not in the unconscious where the pleasure principle sees wish and act, desire and deed, as one and the same thing. Disallowed motives remain in the repressed unconscious as long as they cannot reach conscious realization. They remain potential realities struggling for expression, possibly realizable, at least as far as the unconscious is concerned.

As a result, the unconscious cannot distinguish between a mere wish which will not be carried out and a real act which will. This is an attribute of the ego, not the id. The repressed unconscious is in the business of making pleasure-maximizing demands on conscious choice, not arbitrating between them as conscious intention must. It is rather like an electorate which makes numerous contradictory demands upon an executive government which must then find ways of meeting them which are practicable in the real world of limited resources and uncompliant facts. The unconscious knows no such constraints since it is not in contact with perceived reality, thanks to the mental topography which excludes it from access to consciousness. The consequence is that it can indulge itself rather as political parties who stand no chance of actually being elected can afford to make rash and impossible promises which they will never be called upon to carry out.

Magic, as Freud shows in *Totem and Taboo*, is the institutionalized omnipotence of thoughts, but taboos, like personal neurotic prohibitions, are also built on the same unconscious foundation. Because the unconscious cannot distinguish between the wish and the deed, the deed must be safeguarded against by denying the wish. If one cannot allow oneself to walk down a street for fear of an unconscious wish associated with something in that street, it proves that the wish is real and that, in the unconscious at least, the wish is tantamount to the deed.

Similarly, if all human beings share taboos about incest all human beings reveal by that very fact their latent wish to commit incest. As in clinical experience, the defence mechanism reveals the underlying repressed desire. We abhor incest because we desire it, or, at least, because we once desired it in childhood and continue to do so in that region of the mind where time stands still – the unconscious.

Yet a problem still remains, because we still do not know what created the incest-taboo *in the first place* and from the historical point of view. Evidently, what we have seen so far is only a structural account, telling us about the topography and dynamics of the taboo, not its actual origin.

But need we consider such a question? After all, surely it is enough that the wish exists for the taboo to exist; why must we probe any further? Having established that in childhood and the unconscious was the wish, why do we have to ask about the deed?

For the present let it suffice to say that Freud was not satisfied with an answer only in terms of the wish. He concluded that the wish could only exist in the modern child and the present-day unconscious if the deed had actually occurred at least once in the dim and distant past. Following a suggestion of Darwin's, Freud argued that, in the beginning, human beings lived in what he termed *primal hordes* – groups ruled over by a single tyrannical male (the *primal father*) and from which the sons were excluded as they became sexually mature. One day (but probably repeatedly over a long period of time) the sons rose up, overthrew and murdered the primal father out of hatred of him and envy of his possession of the mothers and sisters.

But, in a typical way, this satisfaction of the negative side of the ambivalence of the sons left the positive side frustrated. Their admiration of and love for the primal father – that primal ambivalence which primitive peoples still show in their relations with enemies, kings and the dead – broke through as a sense of guilt and *deferred obedience*. In other words, the positive ambivalence, reinforced by their successful identification with him, brought back the primal father as the conscience of the sons. Having rebelled against him in his lifetime, they became obedient to him after his death.

According to the psychoanalytic theory of mourning and the depression which normally accompanies it, such a process is characteristic of most human reactions to loss. The so-called *work of mourning* consists of conscious recollection of memories of the lost one, and the consequent detachment of the libido from them. However, unsatisfied love for the lost object tends to make the ego of the mourner identify with it to the point where, in a memorable phrase of Freud's, 'the shadow of the object falls across the ego'. Resentful feelings against the lost one for being lost, reinforced by the negative, hating aspect of any lingering ambivalence, cause the ego to direct aggressive feelings back against itself, partly for want of an object, partly because, through identification with it, the only existence the object can have is within itself.

In this way, Freud's account of the origin of the incest-taboo sees it originating in mourning for the dead primal father. With the adoption of the incest-taboo, the shadow of the father fell across the sexual lives of the sons. Now dead in reality, he lived on in the individual's unconscious as the superego. In the collective mythology he was symbolized by the totem of the clan which the clan tabooed, worshipped, but, once in a while, consumed in a cannibalistic feast of repetition of the primal crime and symbolic reincorporation of the lost primal father. In the taboo was the wish, but in the beginning was the deed!

The Le Bon–Freud theory

The capacity of whole groups of people to share a common aspect of the superego provided the fundamental theme for the next major work by Freud which applied the concepts of transference and ego-psychology to mass phenomena. This was *Group Psychology and the Analysis of the Ego*, published in 1921.

He begins by generously recognizing the contribution of Gustave Le Bon (1841–1931) who, incidentally, had claimed to have thought of relativity before Einstein. That he anticipated much of Freud's theory of group psychology is certain. Freud endorses Le Bon's view that the group, mass or crowd is impulsive, changeable and excitable. It is dominated almost exclusively by the unconscious; but Freud goes on to apply the characteristic insight of psychoanalysis to transcend the merely descriptive unconscious of Le Bon to include the truly dynamic one discovered by himself.

Freud accepts Le Bon's characterization of the group as credulous, lacking in self-criticism, not interested in objective truth, and suggestible through words or emotions almost to the point of hypnosis. The predominance of primitive, emotive thinking along with the loss of the sense of individuality and improbability; the need for strong and effective leaders and for slogans and symbols; the immediate and peremptory demands for the satisfaction of drives seen in mass psychology – all add up in Freud's view to a degradation of the ego and superego under the conditions of group membership.

Looked at from another, characteristically psychoanalytic point of view, what we see in a group or crowd is a case of temporary *regression* in which the ego loses the differentiation which it acquires in the course of maturing and begins to dissolve back into the id from which it came. This is why intelligence, sense of individuality and moral standards all undergo degradation in the group; why symbols, slogans and emotion predominate over conscious, critical thought; why the emotional and instinctual impulses of the id become more vocal and irrepressible; why the ego, now lacking its own internal sense of values, leadership and ideals – the superego, in other words – has to find it in the leader of the group.

As applied to groups, transference explains why such degradation of the ego and externalization of the superego is possible. Freud's insight was that the psychological group is held together, not directly by emotive ties between all the members (an impossibility in really large groups such as nations or churches where many members will not even have the chance to meet each other face-to-face), but rather by a personal identification with the leader. The leader need not be a living person (although usually there will be someone performing a leading role) but could be a dead or mythical one, or even an abstract ideal. What matters as far as the group is concerned is that each one of the members should have individually identified with the leader and to that extent that the group should share a common superego. Identification with one another then comes about as a secondary process, based on the more fundamental and immediate one with the leader.

Acceptance of a common superego is possible only because members of the group see the leader or focus of the group as conformable with their own, internalized image of their parents/ideals/morality or whatever. The group focuses on a common tendency of the members to form such a transference – that is, to see group membership as resembling their earlier membership of their own family and the group leader as resembling the parents, either in their persons or in their abstract role as providers, protectors, leaders or judges.

In the heightened states of ego–degradation which can all too easily occur within such groups the leader can sometimes achieve near-miraculous powers of suggestion. For instance, reports exist that on occasions during his more successful campaigns Napoleon could stride into a field hospital and command the injured lying there to stop bleeding – apparently with some success! Today we know that bleeding is partly under the control of the involuntary nervous system, which itself is open to suggestion (so that, for instance, surgery can be possible on haemophiliacs under hypnosis), and so it is unlikely that such stories are completely without foundation. In any event, it is a matter of historical fact that English monarchs for generations practised a suggestive cure of scrofula which, like some other skin-diseases, is also known sometimes to respond to suggestion.

According to Freud's theory of the origin of human society in the conditions of the so-called primal horde the leader can be seen as occupying a position in it analogous to the primal father. This is because ego-regression in the group constitutes a return not just to childhood and the family but to prehistory and the prototypical human group, the primal horde. This perhaps explains why tyrants seem to be perfectly – perhaps even pre-eminently – acceptable as leaders of the more regressed and primitive masses and why, fundamentally, psychological groups of the Le Bon–Freud variety usually need a focal leader at their centre. The structure is that of one pre-eminent individual and many equal followers, all, as in the primal family, linked directly to the central, parental figure.

This would mean that if the primal horde as envisaged by Darwin and Freud was the original human family, the band of parricidal brothers constituted the first psychological group. The force which Freud supposed held them together and overcame their individual egoistic desires to supplant the primal father by succeeding him as a new tyrant was the force of identification with the father. The riddle of totemism and the clan incest-taboos which are invariably associated with it was solved by the supposition that the posthumous adoption of the primal father as the leader of the group instituted those taboos. They ensured a form of deferred and internalized obedience to the law of incest-avoidance which once the primal father enforced by his physical presence. Now as a purely psychological presence he continued to enforce it after his death and reincarnation as the symbolic leader of the totem clan and as the common superego of its individual members.

In summary, we can say that Freud provides a dynamic explanation of Le Bon's more descriptive findings regarding the psychology of groups. Fundamentally, he sees it in terms of *identification* – a dynamic psychological process by means of which the ego makes an identity between some aspect of itself and some other object. The reason why it can do this so readily in the context of group membership is that it did so much earlier in childhood by identifying with the parents, their roles and ideals in constituting the superego (a concept which Freud develops considerably in the course of the book, where it still exists under the earlier term 'ego-ideal').

In this way the concepts of the ego and transference illuminate social psychology much as they did the purely clinical concerns discussed in the last chapter. This suggests an important conclusion too little noted even in the analytic world of today. This is that mass and clinical ego-psychology are much more intimately related than might have been thought possible, especially under the influence of the earlier, predominantly cathartic approach of what I called the first psychoanalytic revolution. After the second revolution had introduced psychoanalytic ego-psychology these two fields were to be directly and indissolubly linked.

Although psychotherapy of individuals in a group is certainly possible, few who understand either psycho-analysis or the Le Bon–Freud theory of mass psychology – and no-one who understands both – could possibly believe that group psychoanalysis of individuals is a credible form of psychotherapy. The reason should now be clear. It is that membership of the group implies ego-regression via transference to the leader. Modern, post-1920 psychoanalysis, however, aims at ego-enhancement by the analysis of the transference neurosis in a purely individualistic setting where the invisibility of the analyst to the patient reclining on the couch and the former's sparing interventions emphasize detachment, objectivity and self-possession, rather than group membership or social interaction. Furthermore, the 'benevolent scepticism' which Freud required of his patients is hardly compatible with the kind of credulous transference so easily induced in the members of a psychological group, even – or, perhaps especially – if it is a purely therapeutic one.

Group psychotherapy can certainly produce results by means of suggestion, just like hypnosis (of which it is, in a sense, a variant), but no one who really understands the therapeutic aims of *analysis* as opposed to suggestion could confuse their results. Group psychotherapy, if it succeeds, succeeds as a superego-resolution; modern psychoanalytic defence-analysis most emphatically does not. In this sense 'group psychoanalysis' is a contradiction in terms and represents regression to what I called the first psychoanalytic period, that in which transference was exploited by the therapist to overcome resistance, perhaps even to the earlier hypnotic method. In no sense can it represent a true advance. (At the very best, it can only be a kind of cut-price analysis-by-the-batch. But who would dream of consulting a surgeon who practised on several patients at once? The parallel with analysis, although by no means exact, seems compelling.)

When modern psychoanalysis reached its definitive method of transference-analysis as the key to therapy, it had also reached a crucial understanding of the nature of mass psychology. Just as analysis of the transference was incompatible with suggestion, so psychoanalytic insights into the psychology of groups made group-induced ego-regression incompatible with the fundamental moral and therapeutic aim of psychoanalysis. This was the emancipation of the individual ego from enslavement to the pleasure principle and the awakening of its latent moral courage to face reality.

Moral self-responsibility is as much compromised in the group or crowd as it is in the neurosis, and so psychoanalytic ego-psychology teaches lessons for social behaviour just as much as it does for individual therapy. If the twentieth century, in accordance with Le Bon's prediction, can truly be called 'the age of the crowd', these implications seem important, to say the least. The fact that they have been largely neglected by professional, therapeutic psychoanalysts does not mean that they are really of such little importance. On the contrary, future generations looking back at our extraordinary times might conclude that they were of greater importance than the narrow therapeutic applications which psychoanalytic ego-psychology has found to date.*

An illusion and its past

Insights into mass psychology like these do not stop short at the crowd or the group, on the contrary, in *The Future of an Illusion* (1927) Freud extended them to include religion, having already taken the Church as a representative example of a group in the work just discussed.

In essence, the situation with regard to religion has certain similarities to hypnosis. Religion, like hypnosis, was either credulously accepted as some kind of mystical contagion or was sceptically repudiated as some kind of elaborate hoax. Influential philosophical and social critics of religion saw it as a form of social consciousness infused from outside during childhood and socialization, or as imposed as an 'opiate of the masses' or 'false consciousness' promoted by the ruling class to subdue and anaesthetize the working class.

*For an outstanding modern discussion of the Le Bon–Freud theory see S. Moscovici, *The Age of the Crowd* (Cambridge, 1986).

In a comparable way, as long as the hypnotic trance was the play-thing of entertainers, charlatans and quacks, it was possible to sustain the notion that hypnotic influence was some kind of occult 'animal magnetism' or purely external control which, if it was not wholly fraudulent, was imposed on the subjects from the outside, so to speak, perhaps even against their will.

However, scientific investigations of hypnotism like those carried out by Freud in the course of his early practice soon showed that the situation was not so simple. In the first place, an accommodating attitude was usually required in the subjects; secondly, experience proved that it was not generally possible to force them to do things which they could not normally bring themselves to do in waking life. And again, not everyone could be hypnotized by any particular hypnotist. This in itself suggested that hypnosis was rather more related to the attitude of the subject and less under the control of the hypnotist than might originally have been supposed.

In the event, psychoanalytic investigation showed hypnosis to be an extreme case of transference in which most of the ego's responsibilities were vested in the hypnotist, at least temporarily. In this respect it was reminiscent of the psychological group where ego-degradation occurs in the members to the benefit of the leader, who takes on aspects of the individual's ego, especially the functions of the superego. Furthermore, the formation of a psychological group is based on a voluntary identification which, far from being imposed from outside, originates within the ego and its capacity for transference.

Freud argued exactly the same case for religion. Here too, he believed, transference led individuals to see religion as unconsciously reminiscent of infantile situations, especially of relationships with the parents. The length and complexity of human childhood means that children are dependent on their parents for many years to provide their basic needs and to protect, regulate and instruct them. Because they inevitably tend to see the parents as more powerful, more knowledgeable and more significant than themselves, a tendency persists for later experiences of need to recall this infantile perception. In Freud's view primitive men and women, faced with a hostile world which they could barely understand and certainly could not control to any significant extent, fell back on the pleasure principle to provide them with a panacea: God, Fate or magic would do for them what they could not do for themselves. Like children calling for their lost parents to save them, primeval man called on the divinities to save his soul.

Even the individual in an advanced civilization has cause to resent the reality principle and to wish in a similar way for the consolations of the parents who in religious guise fulfil their infantile role as all-powerful, all-knowing and ever-present deities of various kinds. Such deities provide, protect, control and instruct, just as the parents did in childhood and especially in those respects in which the parents did: they succour the individual who intercedes with them and they perform an all-important role as moral legislators and conscientious judges. As such, they become fantasized embodiments of the superego and perform its individual functions on a collective scale. Furthermore, since the pleasure principle cannot, even in fantasy, procure immediate correction of the ills of existence, it postpones them to the indefinite future, to an 'after-life' where individuals will get a just reward for the frustrations, injustices and discomforts which they have suffered here below.

To the extent that religion is such a transference of infantile attitudes into adult life it looks very much like the transference neurosis. It is a collective transference neurosis which, like individual neuroses, has been constructed by the pleasure principle and, like Lucy's hysteria, it represents something of a collective failure of human moral courage. This is because in Freud's view it is the reality principle enshrined above all in reason, science and technology which should guide us in our undertakings with the outside world, not emotional attitudes which make us want to return to childhood rather than face the painful choices of adult life.

Freud's attitude to religion was the same as his attitude to neurosis – both represented inhibition in the development of the ego, regression to childhood and dominance of the pleasure principle. Just as he wished that analytic insights might lead the neurotic to substitute rational, conscious choices among hard realities for irrational, unconscious repressions and defence mechanisms designed to avoid those very choices, so he hoped that human beings as a whole might increasingly come to prefer reason, rationality and reality to faith, fantasy and fanaticism.

Here, as in his clinical practice, he sought to waken human beings to the latent moral heroism which was within them; but in the context of mass psychology the moral courage in question was that which could overcome the wish-fulfilments of religion and magic with the realism of science. In founding a scientific psychology which could explain this very process in terms of concepts like transference and ego-psychology, he found the moral courage within himself to make what he clearly hoped would be a decisive contribution. By remorselessly pursuing the pleasure principle to its ultimate hiding place in the unconsious he attempted to carry the reality principle to its final victory and the ego to its greatest triumph – the mastery of the id through the understanding of reality.

Revolution, reaction and reality

By comparison with this austere, heroic and objective attitude to the id, that of Gross and his descendants seems self-indulgent, slip-shod and subjective. A whole tradition of revolutionary, anarchistic or Marxist ideologists has attempted to make use of the earlier, id-analytic and predominantly cathartic approach of the first period of psychoanalysis to preach liberation of the id, almost at any cost.

It is not hard to see from the foregoing account that this has nothing to do with Freud's attitude to psychoanalysis and still less with the second, mature psychoanalytic approach based on the theory of transference, ego-psychology and defence-analysis. Most of these predominantly socialist and utopian thinkers seem to have failed to learn the lesson of post-World War I psychoanalysis and to have naively believed that the liberation of the id is the road to perfect freedom.

Freud's own attitude to the problem of personal freedom and the role of the instincts in society is most clearly and definitively set out in his work *Civilization and Its Discontents*, published in 1930. In its pages he reflects on the impossibility of utopias, observing that an ineradicable conflict must always exist in society between the aggressive and libidinal drives of the individual's id and the constraints of civilized existence which always dictate some inhibition of individual instinctual gratification.

He criticizes socialist utopians for the naive belief that the abolition of private property or class distinctions could change human nature. Unlike Marx, Rousseau and many other ideologists of a similar romantic and idealistic bent, Freud denies that man is basically good but corrupted by society. The essential argument of *Civilization and Its Discontents* is that the id is basically anti-social and only civilized by the interventions of the ego. The revolutionary, socialistic desire to sweep away repression of each and any kind can hardly be expected to lead to a utopia. On the contrary, from this point of view it is more likely to lead to disaster, not only through the inherent danger of uncontrolled liberation of the id, but also through that of regression of the ego in mass movements dominated by ruthless leaders and destructive drives.

Yet we should not conclude from this that Freud was any kind of conservative. If utopian revolutionaries favour collective id-solutions to human problems and preach doctrines of psychological optimism about human nature to justify them, then conservatives usually favour superego-resolutions backed up by pessimistic social criticism of contemporary conditions which proclaims the virtues of tradition and the values of the past. While guilt is a pathological symptom to be exorcized by liberation and enlightenment for the revolutionaries, for the reactionaries guilt has a positive value as the guarantor of civilization. For the reactionaries, with their superego-resolutions of human problems, sublimation and identification with traditional values and cultural heroes constitute the path to salvation, just as the overthrowing of those very things is the panacea offered by the revolutionaries.

Like regressive group-identifications, the superego and its cultural heroes and traditional values are transferences from childhood relations with the parents. Such modifications of the ego implicitly serve the pleasure principle. Indeed, both are superego-resolutions in essence. In so far as traditional cultural values and the leaders who represent them act in accordance with it, the reality principle will, as it were, enter on the back of the pleasure principle, which will facilitate the transferences in question in the first place. By these means the ego may serve the reality principle at secondhand. But there is really nothing to guarantee that it will; especially since, in the modern world, rapid social and technological change can render once-realistic values of dubious relevance. Furthermore, there is no particular reason why traditional, conservative values should be any more reasonable and realistic than those of revolutionaries.

Indeed, reactionary utopias which seek to restore some golden age of the past are just as common and just as seductive as revolutionary ones which attempt to create unprecedented ones in the future. In so far as transference serves the interests of the unconscious and the id, superego-solutions are only id-resolutions which have taken account of transferences to modify the ego, not necessarily in the interests of the reality principle.

If, as I argued earlier, Freud's ideal was an ego-resolution of psychological conflict, then such resolutions can be applied to the fundamental conflict between individual and social existence just as surely as they can to the private, internal conflicts of neurotics. Indeed, to the extent that culture is a collective neurosis, the parallel is exact and compelling.

If civilization inevitably connotes some measure of discontent because individuals have to inhibit their egoism and desire for their personal well-being in the interests of a social existence, it would be better if individuals did so consciously and rationally, rather than unconsciously and irrationally through group-induced regression, external coercion, or whatever. If the fundamental aim of psycho-analytic therapy is to replace unconsciously motivated, irrational, neurotic misery with ordinary human unhappiness, as Freud said it indeed was, then the implication of his social theory is the replacement of uncomprehending, involuntary discontent with willing acceptance of the necessity of some frustration of one's id in the interests of one's ego's need to live in a community.

In short, Freud advocated no utopian panacea for social ills, but obedience to the reality principle in place of enslavement to the illusions spawned by the pleasure principle as applied to social life. Consequently, his own position was one favouring neither revolution nor reaction but realism as the solution to the problem of civilization and its inevitable discontents. As we shall see in the next chapter, the radical individualism to which the psycho-analytic theory of groups leads was to put it decisively out of fashion for the greater part of the age of the crowd.

8

Psychoanalysis in the Age of the Crowd

Einstein/Freud ambivalence

Although few would doubt that Einstein and Freud were two of the most outstanding intellects of the twentieth century, a notable ambivalence is detectable in modern attitudes towards both of them. For instance, in the case of Einstein, it was commonplace until very recently to disparage the project to which he devoted the greater, later part of his life. This was his attempt to find the so-called *unified field theory* which would integrate the hitherto irreconcilable forces of gravity on the one hand and electro-magnetism on the other.

Indeed, until the 1970s the situation was even worse because Einstein's greatest and most undoubted achievement, his general theory of relativity, stood as a masterpiece apparently outside the mainstream of twentieth-century physics. The latter was dominated by quantum mechanics, a non-deterministic, statistical description of microscopic events in terms of electro-magnetism. General relativity, by contrast, was a classically deterministic approach applied to the universe as a whole and was principally a theory of gravitation. Notoriously difficult to manipulate in its mathematical aspects and apparently unconnected with the other great advance in twentieth-century physics, general relativity languished in a state of splendid isolation, respected from afar by most physicists, but, until very recently, generally ignored.

Einstein's refusal to accept that indeterminacy was anything more than an admission of human ignorance about reality rather than an intrinsic aspect of it, as the dominant school of thought in quantum mechanics held, made him seem at best somewhat eccentric, at worst stubbornly old-fashioned and wrong-headed. Even today, it is customary to write off this aspect of the twentieth century's greatest scientist as unworthy of respect, rather as we regard Isaac Newton's dabbling in alchemy or biblical prophecy to be a blot on his scientific reputation. Whether future centuries will agree with us remains to be seen, but even limited knowledge of the history of science is enough to suggest caution.

If anything, one might criticize Einstein – as he did himself on one occasion – for being insufficiently stubborn and lacking in confidence in his own greatest achievement. In the period during and immediately after World War I, when first formulating the equations for his general theory, Einstein found that it indicated an expanding, as opposed to static, universe. At that time, when the existence of other galaxies was still unconfirmed, there appeared to be no evidence that the universe as a whole was anything but static. Observations of our immediate neighbourhood in space – our own galaxy – showed no such expansion.

The consequence of this was that Einstein committed what he himself later regarded as the greatest scientific blunder of his career when he arbitrarily introduced a mathematical term to redress the balance of his equations and make the universe static, rather than dynamic. When, in the late 1920s, the observations of Hubble showed that other galaxies outside our own did exist and that they were receding from us at speeds proportional to their distances, Einstein had good reason to regret his hasty decision against his own theory in favour of the apparent facts. Had he refused to compromise his theory, the conception of an expanding universe, arrived at purely by theoretical and mathematical deduction, would have been one of the most sensational predictive triumphs in the whole history of science and the crowning glory of Einstein's achievement.

It seems to me that an arresting parallel can be drawn with Freud in this respect. Like Einstein, Freud is viewed with widespread ambivalence – although it is even more vituperative in his case. Like Einstein, he is commonly regarded as a die-hard determinist, stubbornly holding to out-dated and irrelevant views, out of step with his times and discredited by the dominant consensus. The fact that the same could be said about most other great innovators in science, at least within the first half-century or so of their major work, does not lessen the force of the parallel, even if it does suggest that the history of science should make us cautious about assuming that roughly contemporary views of scientific revolutionaries are anything other than mis-leading.

In fact, the parallel is a lot closer than it seems if we notice that Freud's second great revolutionary insight – that relat-ing to transference, mass and ego-psychology – seems to correspond quite nicely to Einstein's second, general version of relativity, and was developed at much the same time. Furthermore, it was these second, definitive versions of their respective scientific revolutions which were most characteristic of their creators.

There is a sense in which what I called the first psychoanalytic revolution was in part the work of Breuer, just as part of the fundamental idea of special relativity had already been given a mathematical expression in what has ever since been known as the *Lorentz transformation* after Hendrick Lorentz, who discovered it. Yet no one anticipa-ted Einstein in his general theory of relativity, which is widely regarded as one of the most original scientific insights of all time. Similarly, it is my belief that it is the second, post-World War I version of psychoanalysis which is most distinctive of Freud and which contains his most original and valuable ideas. Such insights into ego-psychology and transference, like general relativity, opened up a new field of applications to large-scale phenomena – in the case of psychoanalysis, mass psychology and the psychoanalysis of culture in general.

Furthermore, just as general relativity was largely ignored and regarded with a mixture of awe and incomprehension by many physicists at least until the mid-1960s, so Freud's mass psychology was routinely avoided and treated with an even more condescending attitude by most clinical analysts. What the leading French social psychologist Serge Moscovici has called 'the black books of Dr Freud' were ignored to the point that one of them, a biography of Woodrow Wilson jointly written with the American ambassador to Vienna, William Bullitt, was never included in *The Standard Edition* of the ostensibly *Complete Psychological Works of Sigmund Freud*, despite the fact that its existence had long been known and it was published elsewhere before *The Standard Edition* was complete. In the eyes of many clinical analysts the works of Freud which apply psychoanalytic insights to society, religion and history are at best regarded as interesting side-issues, at worst as the largely worthless speculations of a tired, sick and increasingly dotty old man.

Yet if Einstein lived to regret bending his theory to fit currently accepted 'facts', Freud, were he alive today, could feel some considerable self-satisfaction at not having done so in the comparable instance – the psychoanalytic equivalent of relativistic cosmology, Freud's theory of the origins of the social universe.

The creed of the crowd

Analogously with Einstein's general relativity, Freud's mass psychology predicted the astonishing possibility of a dynamic, psychological model of social evolution completely counter to the static, sociological view which was just beginning to become the orthodox one at the time Freud put it forward.

Between the end of World War I and up until very recently, Western behavioural science has been dominated by doctrines of static environmental determinism. These took two forms in the human sciences. In psychology, behaviourism taught that the organism could be conditioned to more or less any response by suitable stimuli; in the social sciences, cultural determinism held sway.

This doctrine alleged that human beings were largely conditioned, not by the individual, cognitive, reward-reinforced mechanisms conceived by behaviourism, so much as by social factors which established their influence over individuals predominantly during so-called *socialization*. The best-selling anthropological accounts of Margaret Mead (1902–1978) and the influential doctrines of Bronislaw Malinowski (1884–1942) popularized the view that human beings were the products of social conditioning, rather than biological determinants or the kind of dynamic psychology described by Freud.

The fact, for instance, that Margaret Mead's *Coming of Age in Samoa* (1928) became an almost instant best-seller immediately suggests that it may have appealed more to the pleasure principle than the realism of its readers, an impression strongly reinforced by its novelistic style and re-assuring content. In essence, the romantic, South Sea paradise which she described in the book was a contradiction of the view of the id and ego and their relations with civilization which Freud was to publish soon after in *Civilization and Its Discontents*.

Mead paints a highly impressionistic picture of a relaxed society without stress or conflict between children and parents, sexual partners or peers; one in which rape, conflict and crime were practically unknown; in which adolescence was unproblematic, competitiveness absent; and in which a general peace, harmony and happiness reigned, unalloyed by the stress and suffering which is the lot of most of mankind. Perhaps more than anything, the picture of free, easy and permissive sexual relations caught the imagination of readers and suggested that indulgent, unauthoritarian child-rearing could do much to bring about the almost ideal society which Mead implied she had found.

For his part, Malinowski alleged that the Oedipus complex was an artifact of Western, patriarchal culture and that in the matrilineal Trobriand Islands (where descent runs through the female, rather than the male, line and where the mother's brother is something of an authority-figure), happy, relaxed and unauthoritarian relations between a boy and his father replaced the Oedipal relation found in the West. Not surprisingly, he was unstinting in his praise and support of Margaret Mead.

Almost immediately, the views of Mead, Malinowski and others of similar outlook became part of the Western cultural mythology. The doctrines of cultural determinism became widely accepted and excluded any kind of consideration of innate, biological determinants of behaviour, or of dynamic psychology. Since culture, rather than nature, was now believed to determine everything, cultural causes were found for every ill and social solutions offered for most of them.

Now criminals were seen as the products of bad housing, unemployment, incorrect socialization or even arbitrary social 'labelling'; insanity was generally caused by society and primarily by the family; suicide by too little or too much social solidarity; educational failure by the wrong linguistic code; ethnic problems by cultural conditioning; inequality was caused by, rather than caused, social stratification; some even claimed that sexual identity was the result of arbitrary social attitudes absorbed from parents, the mass media or from peers. All forms of socialization and cultural influence were imagined to have compelling powers; advertising was credited with creating the consumer society; 'brain-washing' could bring about profound changes in character; the home environment was given a decisive status in anything to do with the young.

Any fact which did not fit the expectations of the theory

could be conveniently explained away as having some hidden or 'latent' social function or being the product of a collective 'false consciousness' known only to sociologists. In effect cultural determinism degenerated into a modern social Panglossianism: a doctrine which explained everything as existing for the best – or, in the more radical, Marxist version, the worst – possible society. Only cultural determinism itself was an exception to the rule that society conditioned everything so that it added a notable logical incongruity (not to mention arrogance) to its claims.

Society as a whole was imagined to be the product of itself so that, for a while, every problem seemed to have social causes and every answer was looked for in society itself. Even in economics, the aggregate demand and supply approach of Keynes predominated over the more individualistic point of view of classical economic theory. In social policy and government in general pressure groups, regulatory commissions and bureaucracies of every kind proliferated. The individual seemed increasingly to count for nothing in a world where Le Bon's prediction appeared to have come true: the twentieth century was indeed the age of the crowd.

In this uncongenial atmosphere psychoanalysis retreated into itself. Analysts limited their horizons to the consulting room and their contacts largely to members of their own profession. As a purely individual approach, psychoanalysis began to go out of fashion and new therapeutic crazes increasingly centred on group, rather than individual, psychotherapy. In the wider society Mead and Malinowski, and many others like them, were believed to have discredited Freud, who, increasingly like Einstein, began to look like an outsider. Having actually spent slightly more of his life in the nineteenth century, he seemed to have no part to play in the twentieth.

To the extent that Freud was noticed – and, inevitably, it was hard not to notice him – his works were systematically reinterpreted to fit the dominant cultural-determinist ideology. Sociologists in particular almost totally ignored his writings on mass psychology and instead tried to treat Freud as if he were yet another cultural determinist. Those who did not ignore him completely seized on what they thought was his theory of child-development to show how socialization came about.

Unfortunately, in doing so they completely missed the point. As I have argued repeatedly – mainly because of this tendency to reinterpret Freud as a social determinist – the fundamental concept of psychoanalysis is *dynamic*, not static. It is most emphatically not the doctrine of passive, home-environmental determinism that it has been made out to be. Freudian child-development is not a doctrine of passive socialization, a one-sided assault on the personality of the child by the parents, class and culture. On the contrary, the whole point is that children are not helpless victims of conditioning, but active participants who contribute as much – and, probably, much more – than they take from the environment around them.

In the context of physical and mental disability it has recently become the norm to adopt the humane and constructive attitude of seeing sick and disabled people as 'challenged' by their disabilities. Such an attitude emphasizes their own, positive responses to the problem, their role as independent actors rather than passive victims, and gives the individuals afflicted with these problems a welcome dignity, self-respect and credit for their own achievements. The Freudian view of the child is the same. Children are not seen as passive victims, without dignity, independence or freedom. On the contrary, they are seen as correspondingly challenged by their environment and as responding as active protagonists to it. Cultural-determinist attitudes, which see children as little more than psychological putty in the hands of parents, capitalists or culture, adopt a view which implicitly robs them of dignity, self-respect and freedom. They cynically disparage children in direct proportion to the extent that they overrate the determining effects of the social environment and are closely comparable to attitudes to disablement which emphasize the disability, rather than the potential for transcending it.

This emphasis on passive socialization reflected the fundamentally static social cosmology inherent in cultural determinism. In essence, it boiled down to a belief that the individual was always inferior to the mass and could not be regarded as independent of the group. Sociological reinterpretations of Freud claimed that even the unconscious emotional responses of the id were culturally determined, not independently motivated by nature as Freud believed. Seen increasingly as tiny cogs in a vast societal machine or as passive victims of a world-wide capitalist conspiracy, individuals and their psychology seemed to count for little and Freud's fundamentally individualistic approach to mass psychology seemed to be completely out of harmony with the creed of the dominant crowd.

In the footsteps of Freud

However, other attitudes of the twentieth century towards Freud are more promising. For a start, Freud's early battle to win recognition for the reality of suggestion has been decisively won. Partly because the idea of mysterious but compulsive outside influence appeals to cultural determinism, but mainly because it is such an undeniable fact, psychotherapy through suggestion is now widely regarded as credible. The practice of hypnotism, which caused Freud's Viennese medical colleagues such scandal, is now widely accepted, even by the medical profession, and the whole principle of suggestion thoroughly assimilated.

Freud himself, who lived long enough to see this process well on its way, ruefully remarked that it was a bit unfair to use suggestion – his first therapeutic method – to deny the validity of his subsequent and definitive one, analysis. Yet this is exactly what happened. Having grasped the principle of suggestion, Freud's critics then went on to apply it to psychoanalysis proper and to argue that analysis was just suggestion operating under another name.

Inconsistent as this was, it was also encouraging in the sense that once critics of a science begin to use its own methods against it, the critics' cause is ultimately lost. To concede that suggestion works, but analysis does not, is already to concede a great deal because suggestion only makes sense if we begin to consider other contentious topics, like the existence of the dynamic unconscious, transference, the structure of the ego, and so on.

Indeed, far from being merely a perverse and fallacious criticism of psychoanalysis, it seems that the twentieth century's 'discovery' of suggestion and its use against analysis reflects a deeper and more constructive process. It is possible that what is actually happening is that popular wisdom – a ponderous body with massive inertia – is slowly following in Freud's own footsteps, but only one step at a time, and then only if it can be shown that each successive step promises to be the last and can be used as a denial of the step beyond it.

Here the widespread acceptance of catharsis as a therapeutic method would fit in with the belief in suggestion. Just as Freud and Breuer tried to induce hysterics to remember by hypnosis, so they also hoped that they could bring about abreaction by suggestive means. In this way Breuer's discovery that Bertha felt better when allowed 'to get things off her chest' has now become a commonplace of popular wisdom. Today a watered-down version of the 'talking-cure' has the status of a popular panacea for psychological and personal problems comparable to that of blood-letting in the medicine of the past.

However, an even more striking example of the same kind of delayed acceptance of stages in the discovery of psychoanalysis proper would be the recent rediscovery of the seduction theory. In a way which seems to recapitulate Freud's own discovery of psychoanalysis, popularizers of psychoanalysis and modern journalism have 'discovered' infantile sexual abuse and made it the cause of many subsequent individual problems. It is now widely believed that Freud was right about the seduction theory after all, and some even go so far as to claim that every neurotic has indeed been seduced as a child.

Once again, an earlier stage in the development of psychoanalysis is used to deny a later one, almost as if the twentieth century were telling itself that if only it could bring itself to accept one more piece of analytic insight, that would be the last. Yet it is unlikely to be. If I am right about the process of grudging acceptance one step at a time, then one can predict that within the next decade or so popular recognition of the active, seductive side of infantile sexuality will begin. It may well be that prosecutions brought under the assumption now widely made by social workers and others that all reports of seduction by children are true will be shown to be fantasies in certain cases, just as Freud came to realize that many of his patients' accounts of infantile seduction were. In this case the law-court would play the same role that the free association method did in Freud's own development, ideally adapted as the legal system is to consider both sides of every story.

This is almost certain to mean that gradually a wider social consciousness will emerge of the complexities surrounding infantile sexuality. Eventually this will have to lead to facing up to the question of fantasy and the active, dynamic aspects of infantile sexuality. When this occurs the stage will be set for social acceptance of the Oedipus complex and of psychoanalysis proper, rather than the pre-analytic viewpoint holding the stage at present.

Eclipse of the steady-state social theory

The recent reassessment of Einstein's later work on the unification of physics suggests an important insight. It shows that contemporary judgements of someone's worth can be very misleading and that subsequent developments can totally reverse early views. Today no one can predict how the future will regard Freud, but, if precedents are anything to go by, it is almost certain that the third millenium will take a somewhat different view of him than was customary at the close of the second.

Much of the twentieth century's attitude to psycho-analysis is explicable in terms of the cultural-determinist orthodoxy of the day and its basic assumption that the group, rather than the individual, was what really mattered. Yet already that orthodoxy is in retreat, partly in face of mounting criticism of its failure to deliver the goods, in both applied policies and explanation of the facts, but also by the implications of the successes of other, radically different approaches. When we notice that some of these alternatives have also brought a new and unexpected corroboration of Freud's fundamental insights, a new picture emerges which is bound to become more distinct in the future and is likely to enhance, rather than detract from, the present standing of the founder of psychoanalysis.

As far as the apostles of cultural determinism are concerned, recent revelations about the works of Margaret Mead and Malinowski have done much to undermine the credibility of their doctrine and its self-sustaining model of culture. What Malinowski called 'an absolutely first rate piece of descriptive anthropology' and what Mead herself declared to be 'forever true because no truer picture could be made' has been shown to be largely fictitious.

Objective facts as reflected in statistics on rape, child-beating, suicide, murder, crime and violence all tell the same story: Samoa, far from being the relaxed, permissive paradise described by Mead, was in fact one of the most violent, competitive and cruel cultures in the modern world. Juvenile delinquency in adolescence seems closely comparable to that in modern Western countries; and, far from being permissively brought up, children were on occasions so badly beaten that they required hospitalization or even died. Figures for serious assault in Western Samoa in the 1960s were 67 per cent above those in the United States and eight and a half times greater than those in New Zealand. At the same time the rate for common assault was five times greater than that in the USA. The circumstance that a high-ranking girl could be forced into marriage with a lower-ranking man who successfully deflowered her made forcible and surreptitious rape surprisingly common and resulted in Samoa having one of the highest rates of rape in the world. Far from being relaxed about adolescent sexuality, Samoan culture featured an extreme cult of female virginity.*

As for Malinowski, his much-vaunted proof of the cultural basis of the Oedipus complex has been shown to be based on an absurd caricature of what Freud conceived the Oedipus complex to be. According to Malinowski, 'irrespective of nationality and social class' the father is 'an absolute ruler . . . liable to become a tyrant . . . a bogey . . . an ogre whom the child has to fear'; frequently drunk, often brutal and always authoritarian, it is this allegedly typical father who is the cause of Oedipal resentment.

In grossly misrepresenting both the reality of the Western family and Freud's concept of the Oedipus complex in this way, Malinowski reflects the typical approach of cultural determinism and sees the child as the victim of cruel parents and the culture. It never crosses his mind that children might spontaneously, and for very good reasons, have sexual motives of their own, despite the fact that much of his own material suggests this fundamentally Freudian view. For him, as for Mead, the child is the outcome of the culture and Oedipal behaviour entirely the consequence of conditioning. If parent–offspring conflict does occur, then it can only be because the cruel parents – apparently always

*D. Freeman, *Margaret Mead and Samoa: The Making and Unmaking of an Anthropological Myth* (London, 1983).

the father – cause it to occur; there can be no independent cause in the child.

Not only is this the exact opposite of what Freud discovered when he abandoned the seduction theory, it is also, by implication at least, a step back to the sentimental, pre-Freudian view of the infant as completely innocent and essentially passive in a family setting which is dominated by the father. Furthermore, since the evidence adduced for a non-Oedipal situation in the Trobriands has been called 'slim, confusing and contradictory', it seems that the reputation of Malinowski, like that of Mead, is unlikely to survive the twentieth century intact. At the very least, citation of their work now suggests a certain tardiness in keeping up with the literature on the subject, rather than serious criticism of the Freudian view.*

In part, the cultural determinism of Mead and Malinowski was an understandable reaction to nineteenth-century Social Darwinism and to the excesses of the Eugenics Movement which took 'natural' determinants of human‑nature to absurd and illegitimate lengths, for instance in using pseudo-biological ideas to justify racial prejudice. But in stressing 'nurture' rather than 'nature' above all else cultural determinism led to excesses and absurdities of its own. A prime example would be the claim made by another luminary of the cultural-determinist movement (Kroeber) that culture was 'beginningless'.

The school of social science founded by Malinowski, Mead and others became notorious for its bias towards describing societies as unchanging, self-maintaining systems, impervious to internal or external disturbance. Few readers of the works of such sociologists would realize from the accounts which they give that at the very time they were written societies both primitive and modern were passing through traumatic changes completely out of keeping with the complacent, cultural-determinist social theories of the day.

*M. Spiro, *Oedipus in the Trobriands* (Chicago, 1982).

Here a striking analogy can be found with modern cosmology. Despite the discovery of the expanding universe and its natural agreement with general relativity, the *steady-state* cosmology became widely popular after World War II. This held that the physical universe was similarly 'beginningless' and that matter conveniently came into existence spontaneously to fill up the gaps left by the overall expansion of the cosmos. This steady-state cosmological theory was dealt a death-blow in 1964 when the cosmic background radiation was detected. Effectively this was the electro-magnetic echo of what was now envisaged as the 'big bang' with which the universe must have begun.

In a comparable way, modern field studies of other primates (the near evolutionary relatives of man) established that Darwin and Freud's primal horde was no fiction, but a reality for a number of ground-dwelling primate species in which a dominant adult male did indeed control a harem of females and young to the exclusion of other males, including his own mature sons. Rather ironically, it was at the 1967 Malinowski Memorial Lecture that the anthropologist Robin Fox first announced to an incredulous audience that Freud and Darwin's idea had much to recommend it.

Then, in 1970, a study was published showing that, although not closely related to modern man, the gelada baboon, one of the species which most closely approximated to the Darwin–Freud model for the first human societies, in fact possessed numerous adaptations distinguishing it from its own near relatives but closely resembling many which distinguish modern human beings from their primate cousins, the gorilla and chimpanzee. (In other words, the study showed remarkable *evolutionary convergence*: both geladas and modern human beings appear to have acquired similar distinctive adaptations, presumably as a result of subsisting in a similar habitat on similar resources.) Furthermore, it appeared that the only profound sociological differences between modern man and the gelada were the very two features explained by Freud's 'big bang'

theory of human society: the incest-taboo and its consequent suppression of open hostility between sons and
fathers for the possession of the women of the family.*

In 1980 three authors, J. H. Crook, Robin Fox and I,
each independently suggested the same basic scenario for the
origin of human society as we know it today. This was the
idea that it must have been the beginning of cooperative
big-game hunting which favoured the evolution of egalitarian bands of hunters rather than the previous primal-horde-
type social structure (now called *the one-male group*). We
each variously argued that it was the adaptive value of
hunting which might explain the change from gelada-style
one-male tyrannies to human hunting bands.†

Unlike Einstein, who spoilt what would have been one of
the most outstanding successes of scientific prediction with
his rather uncharacteristic compliance with contemporary
opinion, Freud did no such thing. Despite modern myths
which claim that he too discounted his own theory of the
dynamic beginnings of human society, the fact remains that
he never retracted it and consequently could claim, were he
alive today, that the only thing really wrong with *Totem and
Taboo* was that it was published at least 67 years ahead of its
time.

---

*C. Jolly, 'The Seed-eaters: A New Model of Hominid Differentiation
Based on a Baboon Analogy', *Man*, 5 (1970).
†J. H. Crook, *The Evolution of Human Consciousness* (Oxford, 1980);
R. Fox, *The Red Lamp of Incest* (London, 1980); C. Badcock, *The
Psychoanalysis of Culture* (Oxford, 1980).

9

Final Applications

The Jewish question

Sigmund Freud died in London on 23 September 1939. He had fled there with his family from Vienna in 1938, following the Nazi take-over of Austria. With him he brought the unfinished manuscript of what is by far the blackest of the black books – his study of the origins of Judaism, *Moses and Monotheism*.

Readers who, like Sigmund and Anna Freud, are lovers of detective fiction (a not uncommon taste of those interested in psychoanalysis) will probably enjoy Freud's detection work on Moses, which shows that he was almost certainly an Egyptian, not a Jew, and that his religion, rather than having been delivered by God in the tablets of the law, was in fact derived from the solar monotheism of ancient Egypt. This, and the unfinished state of the manuscript, its curious construction and the fact that it represents his final thoughts on mass psychology, make it a fascinating book.

Yet we should not let the details get in the way of the fundamental problem. At a time when world events were strongly concentrating his mind on the subject, Freud asked himself the question, 'What makes the Jews Jewish?' (an obvious corollary of that other question, 'Why are the Jews being persecuted?'). The cultural determinists, of course, could have given an immediate and easy response. Like believers in the steady-state cosmology, they would give an

it's-there-because-it's-there-type answer: Jews are Jews because they are socialized as Jews.

To his credit, this was not good enough for Freud. He
wanted to know how Jews had come to be Jews *in the first
place* and what kept them Jewish in spite of everything,
persecutions, pogroms, exile and all. He tried to answer the
first question by historical–psychological analysis and produced the remarkable theory that Moses, the ethnic and
religious father-figure of the Jews, was in fact an Egyptian
who had been murdered by the people he had chosen to
receive his monotheistic faith after its suppression in the
land of Osirian polytheism. The Jews had seen themselves
as 'the Chosen People' ever since.

The details of this theory need not detain us. For myself, I
am convinced that Freud's account of the origins of Judaism
has much to be said for it, and have accumulated more data
and a number of corrections to it myself. But for our
present purposes all we need to notice is that, in accounting
for the origins of a particular culture, the Jewish one, Freud
found it necessary to propose a repetition of the original
trauma which he imagined had created culture in general –
the murder of the primal father.

By suggesting a *repetition* of the trauma he had touched on
a solution to the problem of explaining the persistence of
culture which had been crying out for an answer ever since
Totem and Taboo had been published. The problem was this:
what ensured the continuation of culture after the initial
trauma? If culture – that is, the taboo on incest and the
religion of the primal-father-totem – had originally been the
result of guilt and deferred obedience in the sons who
actually murdered the primal father, how was this guilt and
obedience handed on to their sons, who may not have
murdered anyone? How could the sins of the fathers be
visited on the sons? And how could the sons be civilized if
they had not committed the sin of the fathers?

In *Totem and Taboo* Freud had considered the possibility
that each generation might intuit the unconscious of its

parents; 'An unconscious understanding such as this of all customs, ceremonies and dogmas left behind by the original relations to the father may have made it possible for later generations to take over their heritage of emotion.'* Yet, despite this promising start, Freud's predominant and final feeling was that continuity could only be explained through racial inheritance of the memory of the deed.

In fact, a better answer had been on hand since 1920, because by following the Le Bon–Freud theory of mass psychology he could have argued, rightly to a large extent, that once the psychological group of the sons of the primal father was in existence the mechanism of identification with the totem-father could ensure its continuation, incest-taboos and all. The fact that Freud failed to use this way out (not to mention the parallel line of thought quoted above from *Totem and Taboo*) probably resulted from the fact that he could not envisage a means by which such an identification could come about, except by actually committing the deed, or having some inner compulsion to do so, like a racial memory.

The problem was that of accounting for cultural diversities like those which distinguished the Jews from all other peoples without falling victim to the easy answers of cultural determinism. Those culture-creates-culture arguments were viciously circular. Analogously with the steady-state cosmology, they imagined a static social universe, one without beginning or end, inexplicable except in terms of itself. Essentially such an approach meant that culture could not be explained, only described as self-explicable, rather like the Deity in traditional theology. Like the priest taking the catechism class who tells the child who asks him about the origin of God that such a question is meaningless because God is he-who-creates-himself, cultural determinism had defined culture as ultimately self-explicable, and consequently inexplicable in any other terms.

*S. Freud, *Totem and Taboo*, *Standard Edition of the Complete Psychological Works of Sigmund Freud* (London, 1953–1974), vol. XIII, p.159.

Freud's dynamic vision of human psychology predisposed him to scepticism about cultural piety like this and made him wish for something better. Unfortunately, his preferred solution of racially inherited memories of primal crimes resembles the crude biological determinism of the nineteenth century as much as it contradicts the crude cultural determinism of the twentieth.

Like Einstein at the end of his career when he strove unsuccessfully to unify the forces of electro-magnetism and gravitation, Freud was implicitly striving to complete his mass psychology in *Moses and Monotheism*. The problem of accounting for Jewish culture was essentially that of linking his dynamic theory of social origins and child-development with the Le Bon–Freud theory of group dynamics. Like Einstein's problem, it was one of unification; like Einstein, Freud failed. Nevertheless, just as theoretical physicists have recently taken up the task which Einstein left uncompleted and have now adopted a very different view of his final years compared to that which existed hitherto, so the future may come to regard Freud's last, albeit uncompleted work as marking the path to the future.

The unified theory

Although Freud failed to bring about the desired unification of personal and mass dynamic psychology for which he was implicitly searching in the closing years of his life, initial solutions already existed in the work of other analysts. Theodor Reik (1888–1969) had shown that initiation rituals like those which I described earlier could be understood as re-enactments of parricide and mourning for the primal father. The even more important researches of Géza Róheim (1891–1953), a psychoanalyst–anthropologist who had visited the Australian aborigines and other primitive peoples, showed much the same but added a new factor. Róheim's work revealed that the nature of child-rearing practices varied with different cultures in a way which could be understood in terms of what I subsequently termed the *polytraumatic* version of Freud's original, *monotraumatic* theory of culture.

In fact, thanks to the recent discovery of a previously unknown manuscript by Freud, we now know that as early as 1915 he had already made one abortive attempt to formulate a polytraumatic version of his original theory. In the course of writing the conclusion to a series of theoretical papers during World War I Freud had considered the possibility that modern neurotic illnesses might be seen as recapitulations of adaptations to earlier phases in the evolution of mankind as a whole, so that each type of neurosis corresponded to a particular stage of development. With the benefit of hindsight and our much more extensive knowledge of human evolution one can readily understand Freud's decision not to publish these speculations, which in their details now seem hopelessly wrong. Yet, in terms of its theoretical aspirations and its attempt to develop the theory of human psychological origins to account for the different types of psychopathology, religion and character, Freud's draft of 1915 was by no means as foolish as it may at first seem. Like Einstein in his many abortive attempts to formulate a unified field theory, Freud seems to have been wrong in the matter of particulars, but was probably working along the right general lines, given the very limited resources of reliable knowledge available to him at the time.*

Although Freud failed on this occasion, he implicitly returned to the problem with the book on Moses. The suggestion that the Jews were the Chosen People because they had murdered Moses and thereby staged a repetition of the primal parricide constituted another faltering step towards the full-blown polytrauma theory. Like Moses, who saw the Promised Land from afar but was destined

*S. Freud, *A Phylogenetic Fantasy* (Cambridge, Mass., 1987).

never to set foot in it, Freud glimpsed the essential concept of the unified theory, but did not live to develop it further.

In essence, the theory states that, as culture evolves, parent–offspring interactions integrate a number of collective, cultural traumas into individual psychological development. In this way the valid insights of the cultural–determinist school can be reconciled with the dynamic approach of psychoanalysis to produce a unified theory linking individual and mass psychology. According to the unified theory, the four principal crises in individual development, the phallic/Oedipal, oral, anal and genital/adolescent, correspond in the development of culture to four distinct traumatic changes to new forms of economic life: hunting, cultivation, herding and industrialization respectively.

The first and most important trauma was that represented by the transition from foraging to cooperative hunting. This occasioned a traumatic conflict between the original hunters – now called *all-male groups* of unmated males – and the one-male groups (Freud's 'primal hordes') from which they had been expelled by their fathers and which had retained all the females. Natural selection would have favoured the better-fed and more cooperative hunters, but only if they could maintain their relatively egalitarian, cooperative social grouping.

Females could be obtained only from one-male groups, each dominated by a single, paternal male (Freud's 'primal father'). In such a situation, conflict was inevitable, as Freud had foreseen. Perhaps it was only groups of hunters who attacked their own fathers and raped their own mothers and sisters who could be counted on to be ambivalent enough subsequently to experience sufficient guilt to make them renounce these deeds in the future. If they succeeded in internalizing the dead father and instituted the incest-taboos on which all subsequent human societies have been based they might have avoided further internal conflict over the females and consequently remained effective as cooperative hunters. At this point natural selection would have intervened decisively and tipped the scales heavily in favour of the new hunter-gatherer adaptation because once having acquired females the groups of hunters would have enjoyed an adaptive advantage over the non-hunting one-male groups.

The problem of transmitting such inhibitions about parricide and incest to future generations might have been solved (as Theodor Reik implicitly realized) by the evolution of initiation ritual. This can be understood as a ritualized, institutionalized repetition of the trauma of the murder of the primal fathers, especially in those societies where a young man is not fully initiated until he has carried out a homicide. My description of initiation in an earlier chapter showed how it can be seen as a developmental crisis based on identification with the paternal values, symbolized by the mutilations, inflicted by the fathers and voluntarily accepted by the sons, of which by far the most common is circumcision.

The omnipotence of thoughts – superstition, if you will – ensures that genital and other mutilations carried out by fathers on sons are seen implicitly as punishments for the crime which my specimen dream revealed in my own unconscious – that of Oedipus and the sons of the primal father. Here, as Freud came close to realizing in the quotation earlier regarding the ability of one generation to intuit the unconscious conflicts of its predecessors, there is no need for racially inherited memory as such, instead, a culturally enforced trauma in personal development which recapitulates and symbolically re-enacts the primeval trauma of the human race.

The next traumatic change of economy came with cultivation. In this case, almost certainly, women played the decisive role, both in discovering the possibilities of domestication of the plant species they would previously have been involved in gathering and in instituting the new regime of child-rearing involved. Agriculture is a *delayed-return* system of subsistence, by contrast to hunting and gathering, which is usually a hand-to-mouth, *immediate-return* one.

With it came the need to be able to defer immediate oral gratification in the interests of having something to plant next season. It seems that a weaning-trauma now became characteristic of agricultural societies and that anxiety about the future of food supplies, so undesirable among hunter-gatherers with their almost totally uncontrollable food supply, became of the first importance for cultivators who now acquired this psychological adaptation in the same way modern individuals do, through parentally enforced weaning.

If the primal event suggested by Freud's monotraumatic theory involved the loss and psychological re-acquisition of the primal father in the form of the totem of the clan, then this second one suggested by the unified theory with its polytraumatic approach explains why it is with cultivation (and delayed-return hunter-gathering in palaeolithic Europe) that the primal mother, lost through weaning, returns symbolically as the mother-goddess of Neolithic religion.

Herding represented another traumatic change in economy with far-reaching effects on personality, culture and religion. The need to safeguard defenceless domestic animals from the aggressive drives of their herders produced a novel kind of religion and a new emphasis on the anal-sadistic stage of child-development.

In *Moses and Monotheism* Freud had put forward the erroneous view that the Jews were uniquely obsessional in their religion in the sense that the more their God punished them, the more they loved him. Such self-punishment by the superego is characteristic of the reaction-formations of obsessional neurosis and boils down to hating oneself for hating. It is, however, not unique to Judaism, but is characteristic of the religion of primitive pastoralists who very commonly believe in a single, punitive sky-god who sends – and sometimes withholds – the rain on which the economy ultimately depends. In what was intended to be a completion of Freud's unfinished work, I argued that such *punitive monotheisms* were characteristic of pastoral peoples because their religion enshrined the central psychological adaptation of such economies: the turning back against the self as a sense of guilt and sin of the sadistic drives aroused by the beasts on which they depend. Such internalization of sadistic drives and their transformation into reaction-formations is characteristic of individual toilet-training, which is fastidiously carried out in such societies.*

Unlike primal hunter-gatherers such as the Australian aborigines who show no shame in relation to excretion and can be quite public about it, primitive pastoralists exhibit considerable evidence of prudery in connection with their excremental functions. Such attitudes are reaction-formations – reversals of infantile pleasure in excretion. Beneath such transformations of attitude lies a deeper reversal of the sadistic drive which is found to be associated with the anal stage of childhood and with toilet-training. Such reaction-formations against sadistic drives are the fundamental psychological adaptation of pastoral peoples, dependent as they are on the survival and multiplication of their herds.

In this way toilet-training is the individual trauma which corresponds to pastoralism, just as weaning corresponds to cultivation, and initiation to hunting-and-gathering. Civilizations, which, like our own, have evolved through all three stages, acquire complex religions with totemic (the Lamb of God), maternal (the Blessed Virgin Mary) and punitive elements (the God of the Old Testament). The son–mother–father trinity reflected here also relates to the fact that such civilizations as ours find the need to recapitulate the three essential traumas in each person's own childhood development. Therefore we wean our children at the culmination of the oral stage, toilet-train them in the anal-sadistic and

*C. Badcock, *The Psychoanalysis of Culture* (Oxford, 1980). For further development of the unified theory see C. Badcock, *Madness and Modernity* (Oxford, 1983), chs 2 and 4.

expect them to carry out some kind of Oedipal resolution at the climax of the phallic period. Only then is the stage set for the characteristic developmental crisis of industrial societies: adolescence and the final, definitive achievement of the genital phase of psycho-sexual development.

The reason for this is that industrialization has had the effect of reducing family size while vastly increasing both the available resources for parental investment in the young and the likelihood that any child born will survive to adulthood. Unparalleled net parental investment produces unprecedented childhood reliance on the providers of such generous care and attention, along with unusually intimate, exclusive and protracted ties with them. This is all to the good as far as the child is concerned during childhood, but constitutes a formidable problem where the assertion of independence during adolescence is concerned. Adolescent protest against dependency on parents is expressed in a distinctive, provocative youth culture, political and social radicalism, and a level of adolescent self-consciousness unknown in any previous type of society.

Cultures vary in the way in which these recapitulations and developmental crises occur, the valuations laid on them and the social representations which they acquire through rituals, myths and religious observances. Using this kind of approach, most of the questions which Freud wanted to answer about the Jews could have been resolved without recourse to the inheritance of racial memories. It seems that it is not so much the memories we inherit, but the superego-resolutions which our culture developed in response to the traumas in question. Such individually acquired superego-resolutions lay the personal foundations on which adult mass psychology with its characteristic transferences and identifications is built. Those personal foundations in their turn rest on historical experience, and the responses our predecessors made to the crises which confronted them.

Although Freud did not live to develop this unified view

of personal and collective psychological development, he remains its true originator because it was always clear to him that modern childhood, like the unconscious to which it corresponded, was the living re-expression of the archaic past. Freud had long realized that, like the gill-slits which appear and then vanish in the course of development of the human embryo, the oral, anal and phallic stages of development corresponded to past adaptations, rapidly rehearsed but then surpassed in the growth of the individual. With the exception of the phallic, Oedipal period, the details may have eluded him, and even there he remained in ignorance of the exact adaptive feature concerned (hunting); but, essentially, he anticipated all that modern research has discovered: the child may be the father of the man, but man is the father of the child.

Freudian evolution

Whatever criticism it may have attracted in the human sciences, cultural determinism has come under a much more serious attack from modern biology. There, as in other branches of behavioural science, static environmentalism held sway until the mid-1960s. Then, at about the same time that the discovery of the cosmic background radiation finally put paid to the steady-state cosmology, a new, dynamic, evolutionary approach emerged which for the first time offered convincing explanations of social behaviour from a Darwinian viewpoint.

Social cooperation had always been a problem for Darwin because his theory of evolution required competition for reproductive success, not cooperation and self-sacrifice. Yet, in cases like the bee-hive or ant-colony, reproductive cooperation reached extreme forms, with sterile castes of workers altruistically raising the progeny of the queen.

But *altruism* can evolve if it is a question of cooperating with the cooperation of others. Cooperation will only be a self-defeating behaviour in evolutionary terms if an organism cooperates with another which does not reciprocate, but exploits its cooperation. Studies of animal behaviour soon showed that such mutual cooperation could evolve in two separate instances: if the cooperating individuals were closely related, so that the genes for cooperation in the one benefited those in the other; or if, even if unrelated, cooperation was reciprocated by each party in some reliable way. The two forms of altruism were called *kin altruism* in the first case and *reciprocal altruism* in the second. In kin altruism exploitation of the altruist is safeguarded against by the ability to recognize relatives (and thereby the corresponding genes for altruism which they share). In reciprocal altruism detection of exploitation may be much more difficult, but, in principle, it is the actual reciprocation of the cooperating behaviour which guarantees equity.

Kin altruism explained the bee-hive or ant-colony because, thanks to a peculiarity of the reproductive system of the organisms concerned, in both cases the sterile workers were more closely related to the offspring of the queen, their sisters, than to any offspring they might have had themselves. Hence their self-sacrifice was on behalf of their own genes (including those for their own self-sacrifice) with the consequence that more of these would be represented in the next generation if they farmed the queen for sisters rather than had offspring of their own. Similarly, altruism in unrelated organisms could evolve if the original altruist always got a return for its self-sacrifice in some way, like cleaner-fish which get a meal in exchange for ridding bigger fish of parasites.

Until modern *sociobiology* worked out the evolutionary theory of altruism there had been a tendency to assume that altruism had to evolve for the good of the group or species. It was even thought that selection had to operate at the level of the group or species to explain it. Once it became apparent that cooperation could be explained in genuinely Darwinian terms, a radical new individualism returned to biological theories of animal behaviour which was entirely in harmony with evolutionary expectations of selection operating at the level of the individual – even at that of the individual gene.

Conceived as the packaging and guardians of their genes, organisms were now seen as existing in order to reproduce, and as evolving if they succeeded. Such an emphasis on individual reproductive success seems to accord quite naturally with the libido theory, as a number of biologists have recently observed. Unless we are to entertain the unscientific idea that human beings are in some way or another exempt from evolution and not its products, we are forced to conclude that there is much common ground between the findings of Freud with regard to the primacy of the libido and those of Darwinists regarding reproductive success as the driving force of evolution.

Indeed, if we look at reciprocal altruism, for instance, we immediately notice that, because one-sided cooperation must benefit its recipient, deception in reciprocal relationships is to be expected. In animal behaviour it certainly occurs. So-called 'false cleaners' exist on coral reefs which resemble true cleaner-fish but which, when allowed access to the client, take a bite out of it and vanish. The false cleaner thus gets a meal but without paying for it by rendering a service.

Similarly with human beings: since reciprocity is particularly evolved in our species and the basis of much of our cooperation, it will always pay to cheat, if you can get away with it. Since cheating pays, it pays to detect cheaters. But the best cheats will be those who do not even know that they are cheating – those who have become unconscious of their own deception and who can plead their honesty with total conviction. In this way an unconscious, repressed portion of the mind could evolve, designed to hide such deception-in-one's-selfish-interest even from oneself.

Furthermore, it soon becomes obvious why it should be sexual themes in particular which are so strenuously repressed and hidden, even from oneself. Indeed, sexual strategies as a whole might be most successful if unconscious, since they could all the easier be honestly denied.

In stressing the importance of the individual and realizing the fallacy of regarding the group or species as the important unit in evolution, modern sociobiology adopted a point of view diametrically opposed to cultural determinism in the human sciences. This approach had stressed the group before all else and had seen the individual as little more than a cipher for it. In adopting a dynamic, as opposed to static, approach to social behaviour, sociobiology inevitably rediscovered many things long apparent to psychoanalysis – the importance of sex from the point of view of the individual, the possibility of repression and of a dynamic and topographical unconscious, even the inevitability of parent–offspring conflict.

This idea is essential to the Freudian view of childhood, and to the Oedipal period in particular. Here again, modern biology has demonstrated the wider validity of regarding parent-offspring relations from the point of view of conflict, rather than harmony.

As long as biological thinking was dominated by the fallacious view that altruism benefited the group, parental care seemed self-explanatory. It benefited the family unit and had to be a good thing. But this view also implied that the behaviour of offspring should also benefit the group in a comparable way. Yet the reality is that offspring and parent can often take a quite different view of how they should behave, one based on self-interest, rather than the alleged mutual interest of the family group.

An example might be weaning. Here the interests of the mother in providing milk and the interests of the young in consuming it might come into direct conflict if provision beyond a certain point reduced the mother's chances of further reproduction (for instance, by lactation inhibiting ovulation). The inevitable outcome is conflict, not harmony, based on the realization that it is fallacious to believe that, at the basic, biological level, the interests of parents and offspring are necessarily the same.

This realization stands in sharp contrast to the teachings of cultural determinism which have dominated the human social sciences and have always assumed that group and individual interests were identical, that offspring were the passive recipients of socialization and that individuals who did not conform to the dictates of the larger group were inevitably 'deviants', 'egoists', 'class-traitors', or whatever. Like psychoanalysis, modern sociobiology presupposes a fundamental individualism based on realism about the causes of social behaviour. It is hardly surpising that, like psychoanalysis, it is anathematized by some for opposing the creed of the crowd with the individualistic insights common to both.*

Beyond *Beyond the Pleasure Principle*

For some time after his death, Einstein's unsuccessful search for a unification of gravitation and electro-magnetism increasingly seemed to have been futile because new fundamental forces had been found. These had to be incorporated in his theory, making his attempted unification an even more impossible task than it had been originally. Yet, in recent years a number of physicists have taken up the task left unfinished by Einstein and, as a step towards what is now termed the *grand unified theory*, it appears that the newly–discovered forces might be included with electro-magnetism in this theoretical synthesis. If they indeed may, then physics will once again be on the path marked out by Einstein, one which might lead to a final grand unification of the two fundamental forces of nature.

For reasons which cannot detain us here, the unification

*R. Trivers, *Social Evolution* (Menlo Park, California, 1986); D. Barash, *Sociobiology and Behaviour* (2nd ed., London, 1982); and C. Badcock, *The Problem of Altruism* (Oxford, 1986).

of these two classes of forces is likely to be very difficult and it may well require the genius of another Einstein to bring it about. As far as the future of Freud is concerned, there are good reasons for thinking that the final outcome could well be that psychoanalysis, so long so wrongly regarded as a purely therapeutic undertaking marginal to other sciences, eventually takes its proper place in what we might term the 'grand unification of behavioural science'. In this overall synthesis the unified theory described above would be an important, but subsidiary part.

Following what I called the second psychoanalytic revolution, Freud attempted to bring about not merely a unification of mass and individual psychology, but also laboured on an even greater task: the revision of his theory of the instincts. Implicitly, this raised the prospect of a grander unification, one embracing psychoanalytic psychology and biological science in general.

Speculating that there must be, in the title of his book of 1920, something *Beyond the Pleasure Principle* which could explain not merely transference, but the compulsion to repeat in general, he proposed a dualistic theory of Life and Death instincts as the prime movers of psychological – not to mention biological – dynamics. Like the inheritance of acquired characteristics which so disfigured his unification of individual and mass psychology, the metaphysical concept of Life and Death instincts, like so many of Einstein's efforts in the later part of his life, seems an unsuccessful attempt at the solution of the problem – at least from the point of view of modern biological understanding. In his book Freud himself admitted: 'The deficiencies in our description would probably vanish if we were already in a position to replace the psychological terms by physiological or chemical ones.' He added that 'Biology is truly a land of unlimited possibilities. We may expect it to give us the most surprising information and we cannot guess what answers it will return in a few dozen years to the questions which we have put to it. They may be of a kind which will blow away the whole of our artificial structure of hypotheses.'*

It seems that Freud's expectation on this point has been fully borne out and that within the time-scale which he foresaw modern biological research has indeed blown away the whole artificial structure of Life and Death instincts and enabled us to glimpse a more credible solution to the problem of what lies 'beyond the pleasure principle'.

As an example of the way in which such a grand unification of psychoanalytic psychology and modern biology might come about, consider the following extension of the Le Bon–Freud theory of group behaviour. Such behaviour, as Le Bon pointed out and Freud agreed, often connotes altruism as well as sadism. Groups can be capable of astonishing self-sacrifice in the name of a higher cause; and even their sadism has a collective aspect to it. Such group-induced altruism can be linked directly to the modern biological theory of social behaviour by means of the following very simple observation.

If we accept the validity of an evolutionary view of human development and if we observe that by far the greater proportion of human existence has been spent in primal hunter-gatherer societies which existed everywhere before the Neolithic Revolution some 12,000-odd years ago, it follows that psychological tendencies like identifying with others probably originally evolved in such societies. Furthermore, modern investigations show that many acts of altruism not directed towards relatives – quite apart from those which occur in crowds – are motivated by *identification* of the altruist with the recipient of the altruitic act in question.

Since identification is based on some subjective sense of similarity with the object of the identification and almost anyone one met in a primal society who reminded one of

*S. Freud, *Beyond the Pleasure Principle*, *Standard Edition*, vol. XVIII, p. 60.

oneself in appearance, behaviour or personality would probably have been a relative, it follows that such altruism-through-identification would be the characteristically human expression of something which we have already met in animal behaviour, namely kin altruism. In such circumstances a tendency to identify with the unfortunate plight of others would on the whole tend to promote the welfare of one's relatives, including the genetic determinants for that identifying behaviour which one shared with them.

Again, in the context of reciprocal altruism, identification would serve an adaptive function if it meant identification with the altruism of others. This is because, as far as evolution is concerned, cooperation only pays if it is reciprocated in some way. We can expect that a tendency to identify might evolve as a means of conditioning cooperative behaviour in the individual's own self-interest. Identification with another's cooperation would prompt cooperation of one's own, but discourage cooperation if one could not identify in this way. Consequently, human altruism based on identification could become established as a viable trend in evolution and identification would both motivate altruistic cooperation and safeguard against its exploitation.

The compulsion to repeat an earlier experience, which Freud found went so puzzlingly beyond the pleasure principle in constituting the instinctual basis for something like transference, might find a straightforward and natural explanation here, at least as far as transference itself is concerned. If we assume that identification in primal hunter-gatherer societies would tend to reflect genetic relatedness and take into account the fact that such relatedness spans genealogical time as well as genealogical space, we can envisage the possibility that an unconscious tendency to identify a present experience with a past one might constitute a kind of compulsive awareness of precedent, based on the likelihood of a present protagonist being related to a past one. For instance, experiences from one's early life with one group of people might be unconsciously applied to later ones with their descendants because the latter could be identified with them. But, since the descendants would in reality have inherited a large part of their behaviour and character from their predecessors, such compulsive expectations would probably be completely justified. If life in primal hunter-gatherer societies was much simpler than has been the case since the Neolithic Revolution, one can see that transference might have been a much more reliable and adaptive attribute than it has proved to be in modern conditions.

To sum up the situation, we could say that, starting from first principles of evolutionary biology – those governing the evolution of cooperation – we have stepped up to human behaviour as we see it around us today thanks to a link provided by the Freudian theory. Such a small step for Freud would represent a grand unifying leap for behavioural science as a whole in showing how we could go from the level of the gene, to dynamic psychology, and on to human behaviour, with all its cultural and historical complications and consequences.

Here the unified theory would nest inside a grand unified theory embracing not merely human behaviour but the behaviour of all biological organisms, be they ever so small or so distantly related to ourselves. Since there are good reasons for believing that evolution can embrace them all and since our understanding of the evolution of social behaviour can be extended to human beings also by the means just indicated, a universal synthesis of behavioural science is certainly a possibility and today seems more easily brought about than the grand unification of the forces of nature still only speculated about in physics.

As far as psychoanalysis itself is concerned, its participation in this grand unification probably depends on adding a final, fourth description to the three classical ones outlined at the beginning of this book. An example will make the situation clear.

Because in many species like our own parental care is greatest when the offspring is most immature, the biologist

Robert Trivers has pointed out that offspring might on occasions behave as if they were less mature than they really were in order to solicit greater parental care than would otherwise be forthcoming. Another name for immature behaviour of this kind is *regression*, and we can readily see, thanks to the insights of Freud, that it has much to do with human nature.*

In the past regression has been described from the dynamic, topographical and quantitative points of view, very much as we saw in the Schreber case material reviewed earlier. Trivers describes it from an evolutionary, adaptive angle which may come to constitute a fourth dimension of psychoanalytic explanation. Its value would lie in describing not merely how regression occurs but why it became an option in human behaviour in the first place, quite apart from the light such an evolutionary perspective might cast on much that is already known about it.

Freud's uncompleted *Moses and Monotheism* contains by far the longest discussion found anywhere in his works of what he called the *archaic heritage* of human beings. By this he meant unconscious racial memories which he invoked increasingly towards the end of his life to explain the shortcomings of the earlier dynamic, quantitative and topographical views. Because he found that not every symptom or detail of a neurosis could be resolved into a particular aspect related to the individual concerned, he realized that some more general factor had to be operative which would probably be innate, rather than acquired.

Although this archaic heritage led him astray in relation to the unification of individual and mass psychology, he seems to have been thinking much more along the right lines with regard to the more fundamental unification of psychoanalysis with evolutionary theory. Here indeed an evolutionary heritage might exist, based on a more modern

---

*For a further discussion and detailed references see C. Badcock, *The Problem of Altruism*, ch. 1.

understanding of evolutionary adaptations.

Looked at from this point of view, what we might call grand unification in behavioural science really amounts to an attempt to solve a fundamental problem which has bedevilled the human sciences since the beginning. This is the problem of explaining the exact causal relations between genes and behaviour.

Today we know that genes are the basis of the code by means of which organisms transmit information to future generations. The effective contents of this code are probably exclusively determined by selective, evolutionary factors. No one doubts that our physical form is largely governed by genetics in interaction with the environment. However, considerable dispute exists about how far such genetic factors affect our behaviour. Cultural determinism, the orthodox view of mid-twentieth-century social science, taught that genetic effects were negligible. Nineteenth- and early twentieth-century eugenics, against which cultural determinism was in full reaction, taught that such inherited factors were dominant. Today what we might call crude biological determinism lives on, sometimes unhappily mated with the older sociobiology, which has not entirely emancipated itself from the superannuated altruism-is-good-for-the-group view.

Neither the cultural determinism of Mead and Malinowski nor the biological determinism of the older biological schools of thought successfully solved the problem of how genes and behaviour interact in the human case. The best evidence suggests that they do not do so in a simple, one-to-one way as they appear to do in many lower animals with notable altruism, such as bees and ants. On the contrary, everything we know about ourselves suggests that between the ultimate genetic determinants of our behaviour and what we actually bring ourselves to do there is a complex, dynamic psychology at work which modifies, transforms, re-organizes and translates such innate pre-dispositions into final action.

Filled out with a fourth, evolutionary dimension of description which it has hitherto lacked, psychoanalysis could go far towards filling this gap in human knowledge and enable us to understand how it is that genes determine behaviour and why. As one or two sociobiologists have recently suggested, the Freudian id might be seen as representing the unconscious demands of the individual's genes, while the ego might function as a kind of referee, uncomfortably caught between it and the partly acquired, partly culturally-determined superego. The result would be a *dynamic* theory explaining how genes, the individual and the culture interact on the basis of Freudian insights into the conflicting interplay of the id, ego and superego.

In linking complex cultural behaviour with individual psychology through something like the unified theory described here and founding that theory in the grand unified approach which rests on ultimate biological foundations, psychoanalysis could go some considerable way towards solving the problem of genes and behaviour and provide a badly needed alternative to the crude determinisms dominant until now. Whether it will ever achieve this goal remains to be seen, but the prize is important enough to warrant a serious attempt. If some measure of success can be achieved, psychoanalysis will find its final, proper place in a grand unification of behavioural science every bit as impressive and important as that now so enthusiastically pursued in physics.★

★Ibid., Conclusion.

Glossary of Technical Terms

ABREACTION: The recollection of repressed memories along with the emotions attached to them in the *unconscious*. Another term describing much the same thing is 'catharsis' (see *Cathartic method*).

ACTING OUT: Compulsive externalization of the *unconscious* through activity and without insight into the repressed causes of the behaviour. Within the context of an analysis acting out is an aspect of *transference*, and, as a rule, what is acted out is what cannot be remembered.

AIM-INHIBITED: An instinct is aim-inhibited if it must satisfy itself with an outcome other than its obvious one, e.g. affection may be aim-inhibited sexual desire.

ALTRUISM: In modern biology, any act by which one organism promotes the ultimate reproductive success of another at its own expense. Three forms are recognized: **kin altruism**, in which a relative is benefited (and therefore a set of the altruist's own genes); **reciprocal** altruism, in which the altruist receives a compensating benefit; and **induced altruism** in which, through deceit, error or impotence, self-sacrifice cannot be avoided (as when a host is exploited by a parasite).

  In psychoanalysis altruism may be explained by *identification* (analogous to kin altruism above) and may be a defence (e.g. against *sadism*); or it may be motivated by rational expectations of a return (and therefore an instance of reciprocal altruism above); or it may be self-destructive and, if internally motivated, an instance of *masochism*.

AMBIVALENCE: The simultaneous existence of contradictory wishes in relation to the same object, especially the coexistence of love and hate.

ANAL-SADISTIC STAGE: The second stage of libidinal development, approximately between ages 2 and 4 and characterized by the focusing of the libidinal and aggressive drives on the anal *erotogenic zone* and the excretory functions.

ANXIETY HYSTERIA: A neurosis whose central sympton is irrational fear. Anxiety hysterias are characterized by *phobias*, irrational defensive compulsions and neurotic prohibitions (personal *taboos*) and find a parallel in the cultural phenomenon of *totemism*.

ARCHAIC HERITAGE: Inherited racial memories which Freud believed underlay compulsive behaviour and which represented the psychological equivalent of the inheritance of acquired characteristics.

AUTO-EROTICISM: A form of sexual behaviour in which the subject obtains satisfaction from themselves, (e.g. masturbation), and which is believed to predominate in early infancy.

BISEXUALITY: The finding that every human being is constitutionally endowed with both masculine and feminine sexual tendencies.

CASTRATION COMPLEX: A system of unconscious representations centering on fear of castration and related to infantile sexual theories which see females as castrated males and castration as a talion punishment for sexual sins.

CATHARTIC METHOD: Psychotherapeutic method used by Freud and Breuer in which the mind is cleared of the causes of mental conflict by the therapeutic expression of the repressed ideas and the emotions associated with them. Historically, its use marks the transition from pre-Freudian hypnotic therapies to *psychoanalysis* proper.

COMPULSION: A behaviour subjects are obliged to perform against their conscious will, usually as a *defence* against anxiety.

CONDENSATION: A principal characteristic of the *unconscious* whereby heterogeneous *latent contents* become compounded into single manifest entities. Condensation is a prominent aspect of the *dreamwork* and is often implicated in symptom-formation.

CONSCIOUS: Whatever occupies attention at any particular moment. Whatever does not, but could be voluntarily recalled is termed *pre-conscious*, that which cannot be voluntarily recalled is termed *unconscious*.

CONVERSION HYSTERIA: A form of hysteria in which a psychological conflict expresses itself in somatic symptoms.

CULTURAL DETERMINISM: A theory dominant in social science between 1920 and 1980 which held that culture, society or material relations determine individual human nature.

DAY'S RESIDUE: Elements of the *manifest* dream recalled from recent experience.

DEFENCE, DEFENCE MECHANISM: The means by which the *ego* attempts to deal with internal threats, especially those arising from the instinctual drives of the *id* or the demands of the *superego*.

DEVELOPMENTAL LINE: A dimension of psychological development related to one particular aspect (such as psycho-sexual development or cognitive maturity).

DIAGNOSTIC PROFILE: An assessment of personality pioneered by Anna Freud in which a subject's progress along numerous different *developmental lines* is charted and indexed and in which ego defences are especially important as indicative of *latent* conflicts.

DISPLACEMENT: A mechanism by means of which a particular *latent content* is attached to a remote *manifest content* as a form of *defence*.

DISTORTION: A mechanism by means of which a particular *latent content* is transformed to make it appear to be a quite unrelated *manifest content*.

DREAMWORK: The means by which the unconscious, *latent content* is transformed into the *manifest content* of a dream. The principal mechanisms are *condensation, displacement* and *distortion*.

DYNAMIC: A description of the mind distinctive of psycho-analysis which sees human psychology as the outcome of conflict and an interplay of opposing mental forces.

EGO: An agency distinguished from the *id* and *superego* and at the interface of the perceptual system and the internal demand system. Its principal function is control of voluntary movement and thought, although much of its activity may be unconscious and concerned with *defence*.

EGO-IDEAL: A term later in large part subsumed under *superego* but denoting an idealized model to which the *ego* tries to aspire.

EGO-LIBIDO: As opposed to *object-libido*, libido directed towards the self.

EGO-RESOLUTION: The conscious solution of an internal, psychological conflict largely in the interests of the *ego* and its adaptation to reality, as opposed to one serving the *id* and its drives, or the *superego* and its values and aspirations.

EROTOGENIC ZONE: A region of the body which gives rise to spontaneous libidinal pleasure, especially during childhood or in connection with adult sexuality.

EXTERNALIZATION: Any process whereby internal psychological realities are transferred into the outside world, e.g. *projection, acting out* etc.

FANTASY (PHANTASY): Usually rendered in the second form as denoting an *unconscious* version of the more common *conscious* and *pre-conscious* fantasies, which are imaginary gratifications of a wish.

FIXATION: The tendency of the libido to remain attached to earlier gratifications or to entire complexes.

FREE ASSOCIATION: The unconstrained linking of thoughts encouraged by the mature psychoanalytic method and characterized by being subject to no censorship of any kind. Inevitably, freely associated thoughts begin to reveal latent *compulsions*.

GENITAL PHASE/STAGE: The last of the four phases of psycho-sexual development during which genital primacy is achieved during adolescence.

GROUP: According to psychoanalysis, a group is any number of people who share a common superego-equivalent for the purposes of group interaction (and is therefore primarily based on *identification*).

HYSTERIA: A category of mental illness subdivided into *anxiety* and *conversion hysteria* in which the chief unconscious conflict is between the defences of the *ego* and the drives of the *id* and, by contrast to *obsessional neurosis*, one in which oral and phallic fixations seem to be especially important.

ID: A psychological agency distinguished from the *ego* and *superego* and constituted partly by inherited instinctual elements and partly by acquired, *repressed* elements.

ID-RESOLUTION: The solution to a mental conflict which predominantly achieves its end by some kind of gratification of the drives of the *id* (e.g. a *perversion*).

IDENTIFICATION: A psychological process by which the *ego* associates itself with something on the basis of a subjectively recognized similarilty with itself.

IDENTIFICATION WITH THE AGGRESSOR: A *defence mechanism* whereby a threatened subject identifies with the agent of the threat so as to counter it.

INSTINCT: The prime origin of psychological motives assumed by Freud to be innate and broadly organized into two groups: the **libido** concerned with reproduction, and the aggressive **ego-instincts**, concerned with self-preservation. According to his final formulation, this duality reflected a life/death antithesis.

INTERNALIZATION: The registration of external realities within the psyche. In psychoanalysis internalization is seen as a process in which the subject participates actively, whereas in the social sciences (at least to the extent that they have been dominated by *cultural determinism*) the subject is seen as largely passive in the process of internalization.

INTERPRETATION: The means by which analytic investigation brings out the latent meaning within a *manifest content*.

LATENCY PERIOD: A period extending from the end of the Oedipal phase to puberty and universally characterized by a relative arresting of psycho-sexual development and advance in ego development.

LATENT CONTENT: The unconscious registration of the repressed revealed by analytic interpretation.

LIBIDO: Freud's term for the more general, extended sexuality which his researches made him think existed as a basic motivating factor in human beings.

MANIC-DEPRESSIVE DISORDER: One whose chief symptom is extremes of exultation or depression or violent alternations between the two and which is believed to be the result of unresolved conflict between the *ego* and the *super-ego*.

MANIFEST CONTENT: The *conscious* and *pre-conscious* registration of thought which corresponds to an unconscious *latent content*. In dream-interpretation the manifest content is the dream as it is remembered and recounted.

MASOCHISM: In general, the enjoyment of pain; in psychoanalysis three types are distinguished: (1) **erotogenic masochism**: a sexual perversion in which satisfaction is derived from suffering or humiliation undergone by the subject; (2) **feminine masochism**: although, thanks to the existence of bisexuality, not limited to women, this form of masochism is normally associated with femininity and connotes a tendency to passiveness, and to want to be the recipient of masculine, aggressive advances; (3) **moral masochism**: a *sublimated* form in which the sufferings and humiliations are purely moral chastisements.

MEGALOMANIA: The delusional belief that one has powers, privileges, importance and capacities far beyond the reality.

NARCISSISM: Love directed towards oneself.

NEUROSIS: A psychological conflict whose origins lie in the subject's *unconscious* and whose symptoms represent compromises between an instinctual wish and a *defence* against it. Today neuroses are distinguished from *psychoses, perversions* and *psychosomatic disturbances.*

OBJECT-LIBIDO: In contrast to *ego-libido,* the libidinal energy directed towards an object other than the ego itself or the subject's own body.

OBSESSIONAL NEUROSIS: A neurosis typified by compulsive symptoms such as rituals, enforced thinking, obsessive cleanliness etc. The central conflict is between the *ego* and the drives of the *id,* especially the *sadistic* ones, often complicated by severe *superego* demands and giving rise to chronic *ambivalence* against which the obsessional symptoms serve to guard. According to Freud, religion is a collective obsessional neurosis and its paradigmatic embodiment may well be so-called *punitive monotheism.*

OEDIPUS COMPLEX: The crucial childhood psycho-sexual conflict based on love of the parent of the opposite sex and rivalry with the parent of the same sex. In its negative form, the parents are transposed. Both forms are normally present, although one usually predominates. Resolution of the Oedipus complex through *identification* with one of the parents is normally the most important single contribution to the formation of the *superego.*

OMNIPOTENCE OF THOUGHTS: A phrase coined by one of Freud's patients to describe the delusional power of wish-fulfilment.

ONE-MALE GROUP: See *Primal horde.*

ORAL STAGE/PHASE: First stage of libidinal development in which sexual excitation is associated with the mouth, lips and eating.

PARANOIA: A chronic *psychosis* characterized by delusions of persecution, jealousy, *megalomania* etc., mainly based on *projection*.

PARENTAL INVESTMENT: A biological theory which holds that parental effort in raising of offspring will be determined by the extent to which offspring can further the reproductive interests of the parental genes.

PENIS-ENVY: Probably related to preferential *parental invest-ment* in males, lack of the phallus is latently interpreted by both sexes as evidence of castration and by the little girl as a cause for resentment.

PERVERSION: A form of sexual gratification whose aim is not predominantly genital satisfaction and whose origin lies in the *pre-genital* libidinal organization of childhood.

PHALLIC STAGE/PHASE: The third stage of infantile psycho-sexual development succeeding *oral* and *anal* stages and characterized by a definitive libidinal focus on the genitals.

PHANTASY (see FANTASY)

PHOBIA: Any kind of irrational fear.

PLEASURE PRINCIPLE: Along with the *reality principle*, one of the two principles which dominate mental functioning according to Freud. It aims at the avoidance of pain and the maximization of pleasure – the pleasure being a bribe and the pain a goad by means of which the *id* seeks to motivate the *ego* to do its bidding.

PRECONSCIOUS: That which is not present in consciousness, but which may have access to it (by contrast to the *unconscious* which may not, and the *conscious* which by definition has already gained it).

PREGENITAL: Anything relevant to the *libido* but preceding the establishment of genital primacy during the *genital stage*.

PRIMAL HORDE: The original human social group hypothesized by Darwin and Freud in which the father monopolized females to the exclusion of the sons. Since discovered to be the likely prototype of hominid societies, it is now more commonly called a *one-male group*.

PRIMARY NARCISSISM: As opposed to *secondary narcissism*, the libido originally associated with the young child's body and mind.

PROJECTION: A defence typical of paranoia in which repressed contents of the mind are guarded against by being attributed to others or the outside world.

PSYCHOANALYSIS: A psychological science founded by Sigmund Freud based on the *topographical* differentiation of consciousness by dynamic processes such as *repression* and assuming ultimate *quantitative* motivating causes such as *instincts*.

PSYCHOSIS: A more or less severe mental illness of psychological or somatic origin which is dominated by a disturbance in the libidinal relation with reality and whose chief manifest symptoms are understood by psychoanalysis to be unsuccessful attempts at recovery of lost libidinal attachments.

PSYCHOSOMATIC DISTURBANCE: A disorder in which the chief symptoms are physical, but the chief causes psychological.

PUNITIVE MONOTHEISM: A form of monotheism usually found associated with pastoral nomads which represents the deity as predominantly punitive rather than benevolent. According to this view, the religion resembles a collective *obsessional neurosis*.

QUANTITATIVE (ECONOMIC) DESCRIPTION: One which talks in terms of definite quantities of excitation, drive etc.

REACTION-FORMATION: A common *defence* (especially in *obsessional neurosis*) by means of which a *repressed* content is prevented from returning to consciousness by the elaboration of its exact opposite – e.g. compulsive washing as a defence against anal eroticism.

REALITY PRINCIPLE: An aspect of mental functioning dominated by considerations of reality and especially pertinent to the interests of the *ego* in its attempts to secure real gratification of the *pleasure principle*.

REGRESSION: The return to an earlier stage of development, especially in psycho-sexual terms where the earlier point may represent a *fixation*. In the theory of *parental investment* regression is seen as a means of eliciting greater parental response.

REPRESSION: The activity by which memories, ideas, wishes and other kinds of representations are excluded from consciousness and thereby forgotten.

RESISTANCE: A special kind of *repression* or partial repression in which the ego avoids full *conscious* recognition of some *latent content*, usually at the bidding of the *pleasure principle* and usually in order to avoid conflict.

SADISM: Pleasure in inflicting pain on others.

SCHIZOPHRENIA: An acute *psychosis* allied to *paranoia*, but unlike it in featuring chronic mental deterioration especially affecting thought and language and resulting in severe alienation from reality.

SCREEN-MEMORY: One which serves to hide, but also to allude to, another, *repressed* memory. Such memories are to their *unconscious* equivalents what the *manifest content* of a dream is to the *latent content*.

SECONDARY NARCISSISM: Libido invested in the self after its withdrawal from some outside object, usually as a result of frustration of some kind.

SOCIOBIOLOGY: A modern Darwinian theory which explains social behaviour in terms of its contribution to the survival of an organism's genes.

SUBCONSCIOUS: Although occasionally used by Freud early on, the term is never used today in psychoanalysis because of its unclear meaning when compared with the more precise terms *conscious, pre-conscious* and *unconscious*.

SUBLIMATION: The satisfaction of the *pleasure principle* by means of *aim-inhibited* gratifications (e.g., sporting endeavour as a sublimation of aggression).

SUPEREGO: A psychological agency forming a department of the ego and constituted by the *internalization* of parental figures at the resolution of the *Oedipus complex*. As such, it exercises functions of self-judgement, reality-testing and ethical and aesthetic evaluation. Quantitatively speaking, the superego utilizes internalized aggressive drives as a means of punishing the ego, and *narcissistic libido* as a means of gratifying it.

SUPEREGO-RESOLUTION: The resolution of an internal conflict in accordance with some aspect of the *superego*, its values, aspirations or ideals (e.g., religious conversion or group membership through superego–*identification*).

TABOO: The collective, social equivalent of an individual neurotic prohibition: i.e., a defensive avoidance motivated by temptation. Taboos are often simple *reaction-formations*.

TOPOGRAPHY, TOPOGRAPHICAL: The representation of the mind as spatial and as constituted by various subsystems (e.g., *conscious, unconscious; id, ego* and *superego*).

TOTEMISM: A primitive religion centering on tabooed natural species and understood by psychoanalysis to be the collective equivalent of infantile animal *phobias*. Totemic *taboos* usually also relate to incest-avoidance.

TRANSFERENCE: In psychoanalytic therapy, a process of *externalization* of the analysand's libidinal attachments to include the person of the analyst and the process of the analysis; generally speaking, any re-forming of a contemporary relationship or experience on the lines of an earlier one.

TRANSFERENCE NEUROSIS: A term with two related meanings: (1) a category of neuroses (*hysteria* and *obsessional neurosis*) typified by the attachment of the *libido* to real or imagined objects, and therefore particularly susceptible to psychoanalysis thanks to its second meaning: (2) the re-creation of a latent psychological conflict in the *manifest content* of an actual analysis.

TRAUMA: Any event which overwhelms the normal defensive resources of the *ego* whether because of its intensity, the subject's inability to respond to it, or the unconscious nature of its effects.

UNCONSCIOUS: A term with three related meanings in psychoanalysis: (1) the **descriptive** sense: mental contents not registered in *consciousness* at a given time; (2) the **dynamic** sense: mental representations rendered *unconscious* by *repression* and contained there by *defence mechanisms* and *resistance*; (3) the **topographic** sense: mental phenomena which are located in systems which render them descriptively *unconscious* by dynamic means (e.g., the *id*).

WILD PSYCHOANALYSIS: Incompetent or amateur analysis which does not correctly interpret *resistances* and the *transference*.

WORK OF MOURNING: A mental process occurring after the loss of a loved object by means of which subjects gradually detach themselves from the object.

WORKING-THROUGH: The process by means of which *latent content* made manifest by analysis is disposed of by the *ego* and the workings of *consciousness*. By definition it is a slow process.

Suggestions for Further Reading

This book was intended to complement two others to which readers might be referred in the first instance. These are *The Young Freud* by Billa Zanuzo (Blackwell, 1986) and *Essentials of Psychoanalysis* edited by Anna Freud (Penguin, 1986). The former is an excellent introductory book which concentrates on most of the aspects neglected here: namely, the historical, literary and artistic background to Freud, his life, published works and the earlier, first part of his career. The latter is a book of selected readings designed to introduce the reader to Freud's own writings, with an introduction by Anna Freud.

A little-known but outstanding introduction to Freud which puts him in the context of the development of philosophy in general and of the work of Adler and Jung in particular is *Freud versus Adler and Jung, Discovering the Mind*, vol III by W. Kaufmann (McGraw-Hill, 1982). Although Kaufmann has no understanding of the significance of the 'black books', his treatment of Freud (not to mention Adler and Jung) is unusually objective and refreshingly original.

Two excellent illustrated introductions are *Sigmund Freud: His Life in Pictures and Words* edited by Ernst Freud, Lucie Freud and Ilse Grubrich Simitis, with a biographical introduction by K. R. Eissler (André Deutsch, 1978; paperback edition by Penguin) and *Berggasse 19: Sigmund Freud's Home and Offices, Vienna, 1938* by Edmund Engelmann, with a biographical introduction by Peter Gay (Basic Books, 1976).

Readers prepared to do a little more might be referred to *The Life and Work of Sigmund Freud* by Ernest Jones (Hogarth Press, 1953–1957), available in both a one-volume edited edition (Penguin, 1966) and in its original, three-volume form. Although routinely denigrated by more recent competitors, Jones's work remains unrivalled and is the only biography to include summaries of all of Freud's works known at the time of writing.

Those who wish to begin acquainting themselves with Freud's writings might do worse than begin with *The Question of Lay Analysis* (*The Standard Edition of the Complete Psychological Works of Sigmund Freud*, (Hogarth Press and the Institute of Psychoanalysis, 1966–1974) vol. XX) but avoid *The Ego and the Id* and *An Outline of Psychoanalysis*, since these are rather technical summaries, never intended to be introductory.

The *Introductory* and *New Introductory Lectures on Psychoanalysis* (*Standard Edition*, vols. XV, XVI and XXII and Penguin Freud Library, vols. 1 and 2) perhaps constitute the best of the longer works, and were, as their title shows, intended to be an introduction to the subject. Other works by Freud which can be recommended are *The Interpretation of Dreams* (*Standard Edition*, vols. IV and V, Penguin Freud Library, vol. 4), *Jokes and their Relation to the Unconscious* (*Standard Edition*, vol. VIII and Penguin Freud Library, vol. 6) and *The Psychopathology of Everyday Life* (*Standard Edition*, vol. VI, Penguin Freud Library, vol. 6). Readers interested in the literary/artistic applications of psychoanalysis, as well as reading a beautiful introduction to its basic ideas would probably enjoy *Dreams and Delusions in Jensen's Gradiva* (*Standard Edition*, vol. IX, Penguin Freud Library, vol. 14).

Although not usually recommended as such, I believe that Freud's and Bullitt's *Woodrow Wilson* (Weidenfeld & Nicolson, 1967) makes an excellent introduction to psychoanalysis for those with an interest in recent history and gives much of the flavour of an actual analysis.

Finally, the serious student of Freud cannot be recommended better than to do what I myself did when I first encountered his work: namely, to acquire the complete works and to read them in the sequence in which they were written.

Index